DEADLY REAL

DEADLY REAL

Mourning and Accompaniment after Suicide

Sabrina Müller

Afterword by Jörg Frey

CASCADE *Books* · Eugene, Oregon

DEADLY REAL
Mourning and Accompaniment after Suicide

Cascade Books
An Imprint of Wipf and Stock Publishers
199 W. 8th Ave., Suite 3
Eugene, OR 97401

www.wipfandstock.com

PAPERBACK ISBN: 978-1-7252-7324-5
HARDCOVER ISBN: 978-1-7252-7325-2
EBOOK ISBN: 978-1-7252-7326-9

Cataloguing-in-Publication data:

Names: Müller, Sabrina, 1980–, author. | Frey, Jörg, afterword.

Title: Deadly real : mourning and accompaniment after suicide. / by Sabrina Müller ; afterword by Jörg Frey.

Description: Eugene, OR : Cascade Books, 2021. | Includes bibliographical references.

Identifiers: ISBN 978-1-7252-7324-5 (paperback) | ISBN 978-1-7252-7325-2 (hardcover) | ISBN 978-1-7252-7326-9 (ebook)

Subjects: LCSH: Suicide—Religious aspects—Christianity. | Suicide—Prevention. | Pastoral theology.

Classification: BV4011 .M85 2021 (paperback) | BV4011 .M85 (ebook)

01/21/21

In memory of Angelika

Contents

Preface and Acknowledgments

Really dead. Yes, really and truly dead. It can't be. It must not be! Why? A suicide is *deadly real*, hard, clear, and strikes like the blow of a hammer.

It's been more than ten years since my closest confidante and friend committed suicide. Internal and external walls of silence surrounded this death. Initially, I wanted to be able to express myself for my own sake, and with my words contribute to others' ability to do so. Thus first a blog and then this book came to be. I dived once more deep into memories and pictures, letters, cards, and diaries, reviewed my experience, and once again relived parts of the past. These thoughts and impressions come into play in every chapter, in words, diary excerpts, quotations, and images. Even after more than ten years this was not easy for me; it is and remains an emotional and intense path.

Perhaps my experiences and thoughts can form "word bridges" for others. Perhaps for many who have experienced a loved one's suicide, the stone walls of silence will begin to show small cracks here and there. The aim of this book is to offer small signposts on the path of grief after a suicide, for those left behind and people in helping professions. Ultimately I hope that this book can increase our capacity to talk about suicide, and that the stigmatization and taboo status of this topic can be further dismantled. For this reason, I will tell my own personal story, which many others who were affected could tell in the same and yet entirely different way. At the same time, each of my own narratives is complemented by a deeper thematic discussion, which offers a little guidance along the path of grief for those in helping professions and those who have been left behind. Thus alongside the reflections there are also cues for the mourning process.

I am a theologian and pastor, and in my accounts I will repeatedly address God, faith, doubt, the church, questions about suffering, and much more. I cannot tell my story without these religious aspects, and perhaps they will be helpful for some readers. For others, I hope that this does not prevent reading and understanding this book.

My thanks go to all those people who supported me on this path of grief and gave me new inspiration. In particular I would like to thank my partner, Andreas Bosshard, and my friend and roommate at the time, Andrea Koller-Bähler. Both experienced and lived through my phases of grief with me in those years, did not let themselves be scared off, and above all my partner contributed much to my mourning process through his calmness, flexibility, and open nature. I would also like to thank all those who found the courage to talk about their experiences as survivors of suicide. As a researching theologian I usually write from the perspective of an observer and as objectively as possible. This book, by contrast, with the many experiences and memories it draws on, contains much that is very personal. I was encouraged to pursue this by Prof. Dr. Jörg Frey and Lic. Phil. Barbara Walder-Zeller, and to them belong my sincerest thanks. Heartfelt thanks go to my good friend and esteemed discussion partner Dr. Phil. Jürg Kühnis for his critical reading from a psychological perspective, his technical advice, and encouraging feedback. In addition, I would like to thank the team of the Theologische Verlag Zürich for their straightforward, supportive, and friendly collaboration and the team of Wipf & Stock. They contributed to the book with conceptual ideas, but nevertheless gave me free reign.

Introduction

The origin of this book was found in the street-art image that can be seen on the cover. I was traveling in Liverpool, looking at the graffiti in the side streets, and suddenly I stood in front of this image. The portrayal of this desperate woman appealed to me, because for me her entire expression got to the heart of the emotional state of being left behind by suicide. Despair, bewilderment, powerlessness, grief, loneliness, feelings of guilt, anger, and heaviness met me there in concentrated form. For a long time I had felt like this after the suicide of my closest friend. As I looked at this image, the idea came to me of putting the long path of mourning as a suicide survivor into words, and thereby giving shape to that path. And doing so in such a way that, like an image, it triggers thoughts and offers an impetus for suicide survivors and grief counselors. This idea first developed into a blog,[1] in which I tried to combine personal experiences in the mourning process and short reflections. The numerous responses encouraged me to expand the blog posts and publish them as a book.

Thus these pages tell of my personal mourning process. I began writing from an internal perspective, but did not want to stop at that. I have assigned each of my personal experiences to a specific topic and supplemented them with a thematic focus. Specifically, each chapter is divided into two parts. The first part consists of a description of my personal path of mourning, with

1. www.godthoughts.ch.

all its facets. In the second part, the experience of mourning is categorized and discussed thematically.

The structure of the book follows my individual mourning process, rather than theories or phase models for processing grief. Thus the chaotic parts, the back and forth of mourning processes, the theological doubts and questions of meaning become visible and are addressed.

Each chapter heading identifies the relevant topic that is the subject of that specific article. As a result, the book can be read in any order, and pastors, spiritual advisors, and the bereaved can find the topics that are important to them. The journey of mourning described here covers ten years, and the topics accordingly cover a broad range. This long period of time shows how difficult it is for those left behind to deal with the trauma, the struggle, and the complex grief that follows a suicide.

DEFINITIONS

There are various names for the fact that a person has taken their own life, all of which have different connotations. The neutral, technical term "suicide" is used primarily in media and medicine. It derives from the Latin term *sui caedere*. *Sui* means "his/to himself" and *caedere* has the meanings "cut down, slay, kill." The term often used in German-speaking legal contexts, "self-homicide" (*Selbsttö-tung*), is also non-judgmental, but rather emphasizes the differentiation between murder and homicide, that is, between legal intent and negligence, as is found, for example, in the Swiss Criminal Code.[2]

The word "self-murder" (*Selbstmord*),[3] often used in common parlance but avoided in specialized literature, categorizes suicide as murder, the worst and most reprehensible form of killing. This term echoes the opinion, spread over the centuries, that suicide is a deeply reprehensible act that must be punished by law. Thus this

2. Cf. SR 311.0 Schweizerisches Strafgesetzbuch vom 21, art. 111–15.

3. The word itself comes from the sixteenth century and is a neologism by Luther: murder oneself—become a murderer to oneself. Cf. Luther, *Dr. Martin Luthers' sämmtliche Werke*, 333.

designation is associated with the longstanding stigmatization and criminalization of suicide.

Another common term for suicide is "free-death" (*Freitod*). This term highlights above all the free-will decision in ending one's own life. The extent to which one can speak of "free-death" in the case of a suicide is questionable, since in many cases it is preceded by a narrowing view of one's options, feelings of hopelessness, and depression. The tenor of the term "free-death" is idealizing. "Free-death" denotes a death that is chosen based on philosophical or religious convictions. This recalls, for example, martyrdom in early Christianity or Socrates, who accepted his death in a straightforward and calm manner. The term is a neologism from Nietzsche's work *Thus Spoke Zarathustra*.[4]

In this book I will primarily use the term suicide, aside from cases in which an emotional attitude towards suicide is presented in the personal segments.

---

4. Nietzsche, *Also sprach Zarathustra*, ch. 32.

Taboo

In media, i.e., in films, on television, and in literature, suicide is not taboo. In countless stories a hero figure dies because they take their own life or sacrifice themselves for others or for a higher purpose. Yet many who are left behind by suicide experience social stigmatization. This leads to a situation in which the mourning processes of survivors and the biographies of the deceased are laden with a taboo. This was also part of my personal experience.

1. BREAKING TABOO

As a pastor and theologian, I'm used to grappling with the topic of death. In grief counseling sessions, I have often sat across from speechless people, rendered mute in the face of the great societal taboo "death."

Taboos change. Today, sexuality can no longer be counted as taboo. When it comes to depression it becomes somewhat more difficult, but there, too, stigmatization is gradually decreasing and we are able to talk about it. But death? Death renders us speechless, adrift, helpless. Death is beyond any control and thus at the border of what can be articulated. None of us can avoid the fact of death. As a pastor, I was expected to find words, to have language for something that one generally does not speak about and we prefer to repress.

Pastors have words for death, which are sometimes better, sometimes worse.

But what if death does not occur through illness, old age, or an accident? What if it is brought about by suicide? What if the anguish is self-inflicted? What if just the thought of a suicide makes us nauseated? Yes, then it gets really difficult.

In a job interview a few years ago someone asked me what I would call my greatest failure. I knew the answer within a fraction of a second—should I say it out loud? "Emotionally, my greatest failure is that I could not prevent the suicide of my closest friend and confidante." The professional in me says immediately, "You can't blame yourself for a suicide." Another inner voice comforts me with the words "It wasn't your fault, it was nobody's fault" (and a defiant voice says, "Or everyone's fault!"). In the last twelve years I have also chewed on the words "If someone really wants to go, you can't change that."

Many people who are confronted with a suicide in their close community know this circling, these words, voices, arguments for and against, guilty verdict and acquittal. Yet for the most part these voices remain only thoughts, they are not allowed to be expressed, because otherwise, like frigid cold, they will spread. In the first year I tried to address my friend's death a few times. But people who had until recently been good conversation partners were overwhelmed and fell silent. They looked at me, alarmed and distraught. So I let it be and fell silent as well.

But suddenly the deceased person no longer has a name, no face, no story, she is only the suicide or non-existent. Without a name, there is not much left. What remains is a ghost, an illusion. In all the years, I can count on two hands how often the name of my friend

> was used—when that happened, it was followed by a
> spreading silence. To resist that silence can be helpful.
> My friend's name should be spoken again and not just
> behind closed doors: Angelika is really dead. Angelika,
> that's her name. She lived, found joy, suffered, loved,
> and took her own life. All of that belongs to her and to
> her name—Angelika.

The tension between attention in media and social taboo surrounding suicide is almost a paradox. There is huge media hype when a prominent person departs this life by suicide. We regularly hear of suicide bombers. In the news, films, prevention campaigns, etc., the topic is well represented publicly in the media. But if very tangible people or a certain social environment is touched by suicide, it quickly becomes taboo. Silence, please. Thus it is striking that names and biographies, memories and stories of suicides are hardly ever spoken out loud.

For a long time Angelika's name was taboo for me. Every time I spoke that name, not only did I flinch, but so did those around me. In conversations with others who have been affected by suicide, I found that it was very similar for them. Over time, I knew people who had lost someone to suicide. But the names of the deceased were hardly ever spoken out loud. I began to carefully ask for their names and experienced how, by being named, the deceased recovered the outlines of their identity and their own personality.

Looking back, I have found that it was very helpful for me to shock myself over and over again by saying my friend's name out loud. I've found that this breaks my own internal "taboo." Eventually, her name and the memories of her became a part of my life. To speak the name of the deceased is not the first step on a path of mourning, but it is essential to working against the stigmatization and taboo status that surround the topic of suicide.

Pastors, grief counselors, and friends can contribute significantly to ensuring that suicide is no longer taboo in the lives of those left behind. They can do this primarily by encouraging those affected to talk about the person who has committed suicide and creating space for them to do so.

Who Takes Their Own Life?

Is there a typical suicide? Are there typologies or risk groups? Does personal predisposition lead to suicide? Or is it a matter of biographical events? Addictive disorders? Depression?

2. THE PERSON BEHIND THE SUICIDE

I met the shy, sensitive, affable, cheerful, and introverted Angelika at university. It was her quiet and friendly aura that led me to talk to the young woman in the lounge of the Faculty of Theology fifteen years ago. Angelika looked surprised when I asked her if she wanted to form a study group with me to study Hebrew and ancient Greek.

From this first contact, a well-practiced team and a deep friendship developed. Angelika became my roommate for a few months, and we went through highs and lows together.

In 2004, Angelika wrote on my birthday card: "I am grateful and happy that I get to know you, and I deeply treasure our friendship. I love you, Angelika."

Angelika studied theology with me, wanted to become a pastor, and was involved in church and YMCA/YWCA. She was a helpful, sensitive, and compassionate young woman. I had never before and have never since met a person who was so empathetic and made people feel so understood as she did. But Angelika also had "bite"; she was persistent and had great perseverance, she was active, athletic, adventurous, a good cook, and liked to be out and about in nature. She climbed Mount Kilimanjaro, ran up four-thousand-meter peaks, and raced with me in a snowstorm. She was often cheerful—at least on the outside.

Many people knew this image of Angelika, that's how she was. But this was only one side of her being. Only a few knew the other side, the sad and depressed one. Who knew her self-hatred? Saw the scars of self-harm? Heard her throwing up in the bathroom? Who but her therapist and me knew about that? Angelika had two "spirits" within her. One was public and affable, one hidden and in despair.

Where this monstrous amount of self-hatred in Angelika's life came from, I still don't know. I have my suspicions, but no certainty. For example, only through my friendship with Angelika did I realize how deeply traumatizing bullying can be. Sensitive Angelika was a victim of bullying for twelve long years, her entire time in school. Until then I did not know how cruel and brutal children can be. How an entire class can torment a single person every day, for years.

Angelika was an expert at patching bike tires, because hers had holes poked in them every day. She was used to suffering torment in silence. As a child, it was normal for her to be alone during recess, alone on the playground or in the bathroom, since it was less likely that something could happen to her. To this day, I do not understand how parents and teachers can stand by and watch children bullying.

It is difficult to say, looking back, what syndrome Angelika ultimately suffered from; I knew too little at that time, and it is too long ago. Her suicide was in any case not her first attempt to take her own life. Was it the second or third? I don't know anymore. She had certainly been hospitalized for it once before, but that was before I met her.

Would I approach Angelika in the lounge again, knowing how this friendship would end? Probably so. In spite of everything. I not only gained (and lost) a deep friendship, but also got to watch as a shy, introverted person slowly thawed and blossomed. I also learned a lot from Angelika and gained a better sensitivity to and understanding for "outsiders." Bullying is a heavy psychological burden for those affected, one that can have traumatic consequences. No matter the setting, bullying should be addressed immediately and under no circumstances should it be tolerated. Bullying is a risk factor for suicidal behavior in adolescence. In addition, shame, humiliation, social exclusion, rejection, failure, or the fear of losing a loved one are other things that can lead to suicide in this age group. Other risk factors affect all age groups equally: a previous suicide attempt, suicide plans, lethality of method, physical and sexual abuse, mental illness, family history of depression and suicide, family conflicts, feelings of worthlessness, non-heterosexual orientation in an unsupportive environment, loss of a parent, impulsive aggression, and personality disorders.[1]

Ultimately, despite all the criteria and risk factors, there is no classic suicidal personality, although many people wish for a clear typology. Suicide affects both prominent and unknown people, of all educational backgrounds and ages, and from every social group.[2]

1. Plener, *Suizidales Verhalten*, 62–64.
2. Otzelberger, *Suizid*, 38–43.

Suicide Prevention in Personal Relationships

Anyone who knows about a loved one's suicidal tendencies often wonders about how this person could be helped. Suicide prevention in friendships and pastoral relationships is therefore not uncommon. This was also a central theme in my friendship with Angelika.

3. DEPARTURE WITH A SAFETY NET

During our friendship, I had already asked Angelika to give me all the pills she had collected. She did. But her psychiatrist apparently had no qualms about prescribing her calming, stabilizing, and sleep-inducing medication. What was intended to calm Angelika worried me deeply. I wrestled with this internally, considered contacting this therapist, but ultimately trusted that she knew what she was doing.

Despite the emotional ups and downs, Angelika and I were often inseparable. We laughed a lot and had fun; not only did I bring her out of the depths, but she did the same for me a few times—one hand washes the other. Angelika was my maid of honor, I entrusted my rats to her, and she was my partner in crime.

After my wedding in the spring of 2006 my husband and I planned a months-long honeymoon. I was excited and worried at the same time. Before the trip I made Angelika promise: she solemnly promised, gave me her word of honor, and so on, that she would absolutely not hurt herself. She assured me that she wanted to live. Promised not to take her own life.

Even so, we came up with a little emergency plan, where we made note of what options Angelika had if her suicidal thoughts became too strong. On a sheet of paper, we wrote down simple things, especially those that had already helped Angelika, such as jogging, making a cup of coffee and writing in her diary, watching a movie, meeting up with someone, contacting me, or calling her therapist. I also asked a friend to take care of Angelika while I was away. Angelika had my cell phone number, and I was always available for her (and she for me). As I said goodbye to Angelika at the airport, I had no idea that it was the last time I would see her. As she was saying goodbye, she put a card in my hand, and the last sentence read: "May God be near you with his love, his light, and grant you strength. And I will try to feel all that again and claim it for myself."

Suicide prevention was certainly a theme in our friendship. There is one thing I would do differently today: I would have the courage to ask Angelika to talk to her therapist—or to go with her myself. I would talk to this person about Angelika's suicidal tendencies and question the multitude of prescription drugs. But I also know that I would never have acted behind Angelika's back. Only with her consent would I have pursued the issue; for me, accepting and protecting every person's self-determination and freedom is a central concern.

But if someone suspects suicidal tendencies, they should certainly ask for more details. The idea that direct inquiries promote suicidal tendencies is still widespread. But this has not been proven empirically. On the contrary, people with acute suicidal tendencies experience direct questions as lightening the burden.[1] Here is a list of alarm signals for possible suicidal tendencies that can be asked about.[2]

- Suicidal ideation
- Concrete statement of wanting to die
- Feeling of meaninglessness and hopelessness
- Increased anxiety
- Feeling of being trapped
- (Social) withdrawal
- Substance use/abuse
- Anger
- Recklessness
- Mood changes
- Changed sleep habits
- History of suicidal tendencies

If an increased risk of suicide is detected, it is necessary to take further steps. In my opinion it is essential, both in a friendship and in a pastoral situation, to discuss and define these further steps together. It can be helpful to create a contingency plan in which, for example, emotional, physical, and religious resources are explored and which identifies who can be contacted in an emergency. It is crucial to identify reliable contacts who are available around the clock, in case suicidal thoughts grow stronger. Social withdrawal is usually observed in the phase before a suicide attempt. Spiritual advisors can work against this with their offer of a relationship. In this, an accepting, non-judgmental attitude is essential. If the

1. Morgenthaler, *Seelsorge*, 192; Plener, *Suizidales Verhalten*, 61.

2. American Psychiatric Association, *Practice Guideline*; American Psychiatric Association, "Assessing and Treating Suicidal Behaviors"; Plener, *Suizidales Verhalten*, 60–62.

person has a therapist, they should also be notified. A contract can also be helpful in certain situations. This would establish, for example, that the suicidal person will not do anything to themselves until the next meeting.[3] If suicidal intentions become so concrete that someone can give a time and place for their planned suicide, hospitalization is urgently needed. Friends as well as spiritual advisors who feel overwhelmed by the situation should refer the suicidal person to a specialist or to the outpatient clinic of a psychiatric hospital.[4]

We tried some of these things: Angelika promised me to stay alive, we had an emergency plan, Angelika had a therapist, my accessibility was made clear. Preventive measures are good and important, but they do not provide a guarantee.

3. Herbst, *Beziehungsweise*, 455.
4. Morgenthaler, *Seelsorge*, 193.

News of the Suicide

An unexpected call in the middle of the night, the police at the door. No one can prepare for the news of a suicide.

4. JOB'S NEWS

Hardly anything has ever burned itself into my memory like the 16th of August, 2006. All the details remain, as if someone had taken a glowing branding iron and burned the evening hours of August 16 into my brain: the sunset in Bryce Canyon, my partner's laughing face, my amazement at the spectacle of nature, the colors, shapes, and smells, a missed call from Angelika's number on my phone . . .

I worried as I made my way to the motel. That was unusual, what could be wrong? I tried to reach her; for hours no one answered the phone. Nervous and worried, I kept punching her number into the phone—just to be sure I had dialed right. Finally there was a crackle on the line and I could hear a voice. "But that's not Angelika," ran through my head. No, it was her sister, who handed the phone to her father. Immediately my heart began to race and my hands were damp with sweat. Angelika's father told me that Angelika was dead.

Sunset, spectacle of nature, dead, Bryce Canyon, dead, nausea, the dark hotel room, everything kept spinning through my head. It took away my breath, my speech, and my life for the next few years. Where was the floor, where was ceiling? The mirror on the hotel dresser raced by, circling around me. I could no longer stand up, I began to disintegrate and at the same time a thick gray cloud sank down upon me, enveloping me in a numb calm.

I wanted to know what had happened, but her father hesitated, did not want to speak. Angelika's family had actually called me from her phone because they wanted to know how their daughter and sister wanted to be buried. Since death was a frequent topic of conversation between us I was able to tell them.

Again and again I repeated over the phone that she could not have killed herself: "She promised me she would stay alive!" But to determine the exact cause of death, we had to wait for the autopsy. My internal dialogues in those days awaiting the autopsy report are still clear and present in my mind. Though I mourned deeply, I hoped so much that she had died of natural causes. Heart failure? Or what other reasons for a sudden death at twenty-six could there be? I desperately hoped that it was not suicide and wrestled with knowing deep down that it would be. But suicide—that simply could not be! Not this betrayal of herself, of life, of me, the future, and our many shared plans and ideas. Not transforming from a victim to a perpetrator against herself!

Ultimately I got Angelika's father to talk a few days later, after the autopsy. She had taken more than 120 pills. Did she want to be on the safe side?

One fact makes me doubt even now the finality of her decision. Angelika took the pills knowing that she had plans to meet with a trusted friend thirty minutes

> later. Angelika did not show up and no one wondered where she was!? Or not until too late, the next morning.
>
> I have little memory of the days and weeks that followed the news of my closest confidante and friend's suicide. I felt nothing, floated around like a ghost, out of place on earth. Everything went silent, there were no more birds to hear, the mist settled around me, wrapped me up until I saw nothing and felt nothing. My laments turned toward God now and then: "God, is it true? God, how could you allow it to happen?" Was she dead, was she alive, what was real?

This first phase of mourning is often described in the literature as "shock"[1] or "denial."[2] This condition is not observed in every case of mourning. But in my experience it applied completely. The shock was so great that I could do nothing but freeze up and insist internally that Angelika was still alive. Looking back I think that this phase was important; without this emotional shutdown I would not have endured the situation.

Those left behind can respond differently to the news of a suicide. Some freeze up, break down, scream, cry, or fall silent. The human system is built with an automatic protective mechanism that is useful in the initial period of mourning. It took weeks before I was gradually able to emerge from this state. Others need hours, days, or months. In the end, every person reacts differently and usually they gradually overcome this "Job's phase" (if not, seek help!). In our fast-paced society, even "denial" and "shock" are hardly permitted anymore. But the human psyche does not adapt to the pace of society. In my opinion, it is important that those impacted by suicide are given the time needed to come to grips with the reality of the death.

It is helpful for the grieving process if news of the death is given as clearly and directly as possible (but still sensitively). This

1. Spiegel, *Der Prozeß des Trauerns.*
2. Kast, *Trauern*; Kübler-Ross, *Interviews mit Sterbenden.*

can avoid a delayed reaction of grief. People who are confronted with the news of a suicide should not be left alone.[3] Emergency counseling in particular serves an important function in the first hours after the news has been received. Without needing to do much, the accepting, understanding presence of emergency counselors, friends, or pastors is helpful.

3. Gill, *Suizid: Wie weiter?*, 122.

One Last Look—
Farewell to the Deceased

Those left behind are still occasionally advised not to see the deceased person a final time. There are situations in which this is hardly possible due to a violent manner of death. But in many cases it is possible for the bereaved to see the deceased again. This has a positive impact on the grieving process. Unfortunately, this was not possible in my case.

---

5. ONE LAST LOOK

I wanted to see Angelika again. Look at her face one last time, hold fast to the memories and moments of our friendship. One last time before everything seemed to be over.

Intuitively and cognitively, I knew it is helpful for the grieving process to see the deceased person again. The unthinkable becomes more tangible, even if it is a confrontation with the brutal reality. But there was a problem that separated my deceased friend and me, and it was not the 8,407 kilometers and the Atlantic ocean. When I expressed my wish to see Angelika again to her father over the phone, he closed up. His voice changed and he told me that "she doesn't look so good anymore." That didn't matter to me! I wanted to see her again!

At the same time I felt that now, after they had the information they needed from me for the burial (including a worship service), my work was done. I was not a family member and thus was somehow no longer wanted. As a "stranger," to want to see someone who had taken their own life crossed the line of familial intimacy. The dead body seemed to be the property of the family.

On the day of the cremation the family was with Angelika's dead body. This accompaniment was presented to me on the telephone as harmonious, idyllic, and somehow beautiful. I could not speak! I was so angry and full of accusations (which I did not express)! Now her family was finally there for her, now that she's dead! Now that it's too late to change anything! Now!

How often did they overlook Angelika's mental state? How often had they trivialized her psychological problems? One scene is still vivid in my memory: Angelika tried to tell her parents that she had depression about a year before her death. The reactions restrained, along the lines of: "It's bad that you had it, but good that it's over now." And now they were suddenly there for her, too late!

This vicious circle of thoughts spun through my head, day and night. Reproaches, grief, anger, accusations, bitterness, guilt, and above all emptiness alternated with every second.

I hardly slept until the funeral in distant Switzerland. If I could not see Angelika again—why should I go back? Why confront the people, the questions, the grief, and the great emptiness?

Such a situation very concretely raises the question, Who does the deceased "belong to"? Who has the right to see the dead body again and perhaps touch it?

It is often at the discretion of the family who is granted access to the deceased. It depends on their good will if someone else is allowed to see the body. I no longer had this option and so the death remained distant for a long time. For weeks I struggled with the question of what was reality and what was not, and whether Angelika was really dead.

From this experience, I have learned a lesson for myself personally, but also for my daily life as a pastor and for supporting those in grief: in deaths that impact me closely, I visit the deceased person again. Every time, it is hard and painful to see the body of a beloved person. But in the long run and for the work of grieving it is important to be confronted with the reality of "death." Often our brains need this encounter to realize that someone is really dead. The Hebrew poet Elazar Benyoëtz has found the right words for this: "What does not hit hard does not hit home."[1] It takes time to

1. Grubitz, *Der israelische Aphoristiker*, 192.

comprehend a death. A confrontation with the reality of the death helps us to realize that the situation has changed.

I therefore recommend that the bereaved see the deceased person once again. This last visit should not be an exclusive privilege of the family; rather, this possibility should also be granted to other people who are impacted.

Anyone who does not feel able to go see a deceased person alone can bring someone with them. As a pastor I have often had the experience that relatives readily accept an offer of support, especially in difficult deaths. A confident support person can provide security and help to keep the situation under control, even when a storm is raging within the bereaved.

These last visits are also helpful because it becomes clear that the person themselves is no longer here. The body, which enables life, love, activity, and tranquility, now lies there as a shell. The person with their character and their spirit, with everything that made them, is gone. In the Christian hope, of course, they are not entirely gone, but secure, protected, and alive in that which transcends humanity.

Arranging the Funeral

Arranging the funeral in the case of a suicide is a great challenge for the family and the bereaved as well as for the pastor. Various feelings, fears, interests, demands, and expectations are often diametrically opposed. Not everyone will agree on many questions. Should the suicide be called by name at the funeral or should you speak of a "tragic death"? Who belongs to the inner circle that is told everything? These questions and others complicate the preparations. Often the true cause of death is concealed due to loved ones' shame or fear of stigmatization.

---

6. THE FUNERAL—THE GREAT SILENCE

Dance as if no one is watching.
Sing as if no one is listening.
Love as if you have never been hurt.
Live as if heaven were on earth.

These words were in Angelika's obituary, but they had little to do with her reality. Her yearning for life is expressed in them, but the reality of life taught her that there is no heaven on earth. Angelika was especially unable to meet the standard of loving as if she had never been hurt. On that point she fell apart, as anyone must.

In the tension between illusion and the reality of death came Angelika's funeral. It took place twelve days after her suicide. Seven time zones and 8,407 kilometers

---

separated me from the reality that I could not bear, that could not be. The church was full of young people: students, YMCA/YWCA people, and friends. Gradually, over the next few days, weeks, and years, their questions reached me: What had happened to Angelika? Was it an accident? A sudden illness? Gradually over the years, I said out loud what was not said in the church, during the funeral: "It was suicide, Angelika took her own life." Until I fell silent, faced with others' freezing up.

I read the text of the funeral service that the pastor had sent me, in the distance, for myself alone, over and over again. The tension between comfort and outrage tore me apart inside. I was furious and indignant over the great silence and the harmonious account of her life. Only a part of my beloved friend was buried there and only a piece was bid farewell. On top of that, her family appeared as the center of Angelika's life.

But from the family itself no one stood by her and called her decision by name! It was not an accident, it was a suicide. It was a last cry for help, her last rebellion against a life and a system that she could not bear. A last scream to express her internal, gray powerlessness.

I did not know at that time that this indignation over the silence would accompany me for a long time yet and would bring the blood in my veins to a boil. At the same time, some words from the service comforted me. They were words that let me hope for eternity in the darkness of life. At that time it was a comfort to me that I could hope to meet Angelika again someday and somewhere after my own death. I wrote in my diary,

> Today I read Angelika's funeral service by XY. His words and thoughts on Angelika's life did me good, even if I cried the whole time. I think he got many things right, sensitively and comfortingly. Yes, certain words really comforted me in all my sadness.

> The words of eternal life give hope and comfort.
> They are not merely empty phrases, no, they are
> truth in the midst of all the pain and darkness. But
> it just hurts so much. The pain of this loss is huge,
> physically palpable, I don't know how I can express
> it.
>
> I found the strongest comfort at the end of the ser-
> mon. This consisted of words I knew, of Angelika's own
> words. Seven months earlier, Angelika had said these
> words at a baptism to the children being baptized, and
> secretly perhaps more so to herself:
>
>> God knows all questions and doubts, even despair
>> over oneself. Nevertheless, in all this God says: You
>> have the right to be my child. Come into my arms
>> with your despair. You are my child. No one can take
>> that right from you.
>
> And at the end of the sermon these words were
> followed by this quotation from Romans:
>
>> That's exactly how it is, Angelika. No one can take
>> that right from you!
>> Neither death nor life,
>> neither height nor depth,
>> neither angels nor powers
>> can separate you from the love of God that is in
>> Christ Jesus our Lord.
>> (Rom 8:38–39)
>> Amen

A suicide is difficult to process, and "historical shame" makes the process even more difficult. Relatives and mourners are afraid they will be avoided. Which is certainly a justified fear, since acquaintances again and again cross to the other side of the street or act as if they have not seen those in mourning. This behavior is probably due to the widespread feelings of helplessness in dealing with mourners after a suicide, but also to the historically difficult handling of the issue. Suicide was considered a serious crime and, among other things, led to relatives of the deceased being ostracized.[1] From this perspective, the continued desire to conceal suicide at the funeral service is still understandable.

Nevertheless, I am still stunned that the truth was never spoken during the funeral service, in the obituary notice, or in the letter of thanks. It was never said that Angelika had ended her own life. Thus Angelika's death is still clouded with uncertainty for many. Angelika's life, and even more rarely her death, is mentioned only quietly or not at all. In my opinion, to call a suicide by name is a matter of respect for the life and suffering of the person who has committed suicide. Identifying this reality itself protects the dignity of the deceased.

This experience has moved me not to conceal suicide in my pastoral duties and personal life. The truth is in the air in any case. However, treating suicide as taboo significantly limits the extent to which those left behind are able to grieve and take action. The organization of the funeral service, the way in which news of the suicide is communicated, how it is spoken about—this all remains a challenge. Overall, a compassionate, accepting, and undogmatic attitude in supporting the bereaved and organizing the funeral service is helpful.[2] The end of the sermon from Angelika's funeral became central to my theological understanding of suicides. It is also what should, in my view, be emphasized in such a service: No one can take from a person who has committed suicide the right to be embraced and accepted by God, with everything that is and was. This comforted me at that time because I realized that divine acceptance cannot be forfeited even by the act of suicide.

The family of the deceased is usually the central focus at a funeral service and in the time that follows. But there are almost always people who are equally affected by the death but remain hidden. Few were aware of my grief and my great loss in Angelika's death; I was not "family." Yet my life was turned upside down. From this experience I have learned to keep an eye out for those

1. For further historical and theological perspectives, see the chapter "Suicide in Theology and Pastoral Care."

2. Christ-Friedrich, *Der verzweifelte Versuch zu verändern*, 136–38.

impacted among the closest group of friends in a situation of mourning, and I make an effort to give these people a voice in the organization of the farewell.

In my personal accounts and especially in this one on "the funeral—the great silence," my anger at the various people in Angelika's world, such as her family, her therapist, her bullying classmates, etc., is palpable. I was no longer able to complain to Angelika herself for what she had done. But the theodicy question was unavoidable and the "why" of the suicide left me no peace. I had to find some surface onto which to project my anger and my unanswered questions. In my grieving process Angelika's family and her therapist became these surfaces. Others impacted by suicide might blame the ex-boyfriend, the wife, a doctor, or a work environment for the suicide. Projection surfaces serve to shift an internal, mental conflict onto the outside world and thus to find a way of dealing with the inexplicable and an outlet for overwhelming emotions.

Internal Numbness

Many people who are left behind can hardly cope with the first days and weeks after a suicide. Like a movie, life goes on around them but they are not touched by it. Sudden fears, anger, and speechlessness can be mixed up within the numbness. These moments are equally unbearable.

7. THE JOURNEY CONTINUES, LIFE STANDS STILL

My partner and I actually wanted to continue our honeymoon in the United States. We still had two months left. But after Angelika's death, something in me stopped. Being constantly on the move and my internal stagnation were contradictions that I could not endure. It was impossible for me to fall asleep every night in a different place and a different bed. Fear tormented me, sadness and anger overwhelmed me over and over again. My husband could not leave me alone for one minute without the worry that I would fall into despair. Angelika's suicide also deeply called my life as a whole into question.

So we decided to drive across the United States to good friends. In two days we covered more than three thousand kilometers, until we finally arrived in Dallas,

Texas. My joy at seeing our friends again was great—but the internal numbness and emptiness were greater. I moved through the days like a zombie. The pain was unbearable, despite the acceptance and love of our friends. I struggled out of bed in the morning, only to drag myself through the day, and lie awake in bed at night staring at the ceiling. Just as I stared right through shopping centers, museums, restaurants, downtown Dallas, and people. My internal numbness was expressed in my empty gaze. I talked with my friends, played with their children, smiled, and tried to maintain some cheerfulness, but it was just a mask. In reality, everything was simply moving around me, nothing could touch me or bring me joy anymore. Exercise brought me some relief. I ran through the streets of the small suburb of Dallas, and went to the gym for several hours every day. At least then I felt something, even if it was only my muscles, and could sometimes fall asleep from exhaustion. My partner joined me in this excessive exercise program and stayed by my side. Only the emails, phone calls, and texts from confused friends tore me from my numb, exercise-obsessed state. They all wanted to know what had happened to Angelika. Most of them had attended the funeral, but they could not make sense of the situation. They contacted me with their questions and wanted clarity about the cause of death. I was able to give them the information they needed.

I don't remember much more from that time. But after a little more than a month, my fear had subsided enough that we decided to continue our travels. We crossed through Texas, drove to New Orleans, and then north along the Mississippi. Yet with the continued journey, our return to Switzerland grew closer and closer. Dark, stormy clouds built up in my mind when I thought about Switzerland. I confided to my diary,

I have the feeling that only clouds and rain are waiting at home in Switzerland, that a huge storm will
come upon me there. I don't know how to endure
this. How will my daily life, my studies, my life itself
continue . . . ?

In the first period after Angelika's suicide it felt like everything was
falling apart. Many moments, hours, and days were hardly bearable. Everything was quaking, seemed to be unstable and at the
same time frozen in place. In this situation it was impossible for
me to continue traveling because, in the storm of grief, I needed
consistency and stability. "The loss of a person who is close can
lead to an intense experience of sadness and mental pain. . . . These
symptoms of grief affect a person on a cognitive, emotional, mo-
tor, and physiological level."[1] Strong feelings of sadness, the intense
pain of separation, which is often experienced physically, and a
longing for the deceased person are all part of the path of grief. In
addition, this path is decisively influenced by the circumstances of
the death, one's relationship with the deceased, and one's personal,
psychological, and social circumstances.[2] Especially in the first
period of mourning it is helpful to find small anchors and points
of reference. For me that was daily exercise. In exercise I was able
to be rid of my restlessness and nervous energy, to transform my
numbness into movement, and feel myself at least a little bit.

My partner was also an important anchor. Although he
himself was helpless and speechless in the face of the situation,
he was there for me and stayed by my side through the unpredictable emotional ups and downs. Sometimes I needed to be alone
in order to sort through my thoughts. But in that situation, I often became overwhelmed. It was helpful to have people around
me distracting me with sometimes annoying banalities. It would
have been even better if I could have simply been myself, with my
despair and grief, and been able to show these feelings. This was

1. Wagner, *Komplizierte Trauer*, 2.
2. Wagner, *Komplizierte Trauer*, 4.

somewhat possible, certainly with my partner. But often I went through the day with a happy mask, which took an enormous amount of energy.

Many people are very uncertain about how to treat those impacted by suicide. They don't know what to say or how they should behave around those in mourning. So they prefer to keep their distance. Such behavior is not helpful for those who are grieving. Personally, I found that when I was "endured" with my despair without needing to talk much, when I could breathe a little, I found some comfort. Depending on personalities, the silent, accepting presence of another person or even a motivating exercise partner can be comforting. Some people are helped by being able to paint or write, and others set off on a pilgrimage, for example, to Santiago de Compostela.[3]

3. Among others: Koeniger, *Trauer ist eine lange Reise*; Stülpnagel, *Warum nur?*, 103–10.

Trapped in the Vicious Circle of Grief

Those left behind by suicide who were close to the deceased frequently experience a complicated grief process, although this is not often diagnosed. Constant circular thinking about the suicide of the beloved person is one symptom of this.

8. THE CRASH LANDING

As we boarded the plane in New York, the clouds already began to pile up. They grew denser and denser. A huge storm was brewing with gusts of wind and cloudbursts of rain and hail. The flight was a storm of ups and downs, a tornado of emotions.

No one else on the airplane noticed this storm, as it was taking place inside me. While the other passengers had a quiet flight with a soft landing, mine ended with a crash landing in Switzerland. Back in Zurich, the reality of Angelika's suicide rolled over me like a tidal wave.

I had actually intended to resume my studies right after my return. Angelika and I had planned to write our master's theses while studying for our final exams. We had planned to be finished with everything in one year at the latest, and then to go together into the vicarage year, the practical training year for pastors. We had chosen our vicariate congregations so that we would be near each other and be able to get together easily.

But now everything was different than we had planned it—there was no "we" anymore!

My studies, theology, the university itself became unbearable for me. I could not concentrate, did not want to hear anything else about my course of study, and avoided the faculty building. An invisible wall stood between me and Zurich, between me and the Faculty of Theology, and between me and theology itself. Going to Zurich was so unbearable and associated with so many painful memories and lost dreams for the future that it simply did not work.

With no orientation or foundation I stumbled through the days and weeks. A yawning emptiness remained in me that seemed to cut me off from life and from people. I performed the most necessary tasks like a robot, including my part-time jobs as a teacher and cleaning lady. But my thoughts kept revolving around my deceased friend. I confided to my diary,

> Since Angelika's funeral I feel like it's all over. Somehow it's done. Nothing is left, except a few faded memories, a few photos . . . everything is gone. There is no more seeing, no more touching, no more conversations. What remains is a bit of ash and ground up bone, nothing of the person I loved. It's horrible. This is how it is, and I don't want it to be this way. I can't bear it. "Why?!" screams in me over and over. I don't want to live without you. Can you hear or see how desperate and sad I am that you left? Willingly left!

I also no longer wanted to live, simply to no longer exist, so that I would no longer have to endure my grief. Everything that used to be important to me—the church, youth work, friends, studies, jobs, and hobbies—lost its significance.

In view of Angelika's suicide, my life no longer made any sense. Grief, anger, shame, and despair at not being able to stop her from committing suicide narrowed my field of vision. Before Angelika's suicide, my life had been filled with many meaningful elements and activities, but all of that became completely meaningless. I was helplessly exposed to these emotions and mood swings and did not know what to do.

It would have been helpful for me if I had known something about complicated grieving processes after a suicide.[1] It is presumed that 43 percent of all those affected by suicide experience this.[2] In addition, contact with others who had been similarly affected would have certainly helped as well.[3] I could have talked with them about these feelings and thoughts. But I did not think to look for or learn about such options. There are now very good points of contact for those mourning a suicide. Here I would like to point out Nebelmeer, Trauernetz, and the Verein Refugium as helpful options. Contact details for specialist agencies and self-help groups can be found in the appendix under "Specialist Agencies and Support Services." In addition there are now grief groups whose members support one another on Facebook and other social media.

---

1. See the chapter titled "Theory of Grief."
2. Wagner, *Komplizierte Trauer*, 45.
3. Stülpnagel, *Warum nur?*, 96–97.

Grieving with Biblical Experiences

Realizing that someone is really dead takes time and requires confronting solid facts such as a tombstone. When the fact of the suicide becomes real, words often fail those in grief. In this situation, biblical texts can prove to be helpful.

9. THE FIRST TIME AT THE GRAVE

Several weeks passed before I could bring myself to go to Angelika's grave. I could not and did not want to see her grave, I still did not want to face reality, and above all I did not want to go back to her hometown. But at some point I overcame that hurdle and prepared myself to go to the cemetery—and then suddenly I desperately wanted to go there. My partner came with me. After the visit, I wrote the following diary entry:

> I went to the cemetery with Andi yesterday. I really wanted to see Angelika's grave, maybe that would ease my anxiety somewhat.

> It took a long time to find the grave. We finally found it only on our third time searching the cemetery.

> Angelika's grave is not a normal Swiss grave with a small square garden. It is under a maple tree, without a defined boundary. Two rose bushes grow over it, and

there are a few shells. I think Angelika would like this place, there under the maple tree. It is a peaceful, sunny, and lovingly chosen place.

As I stood in front of her grave with rose bushes, candles, and the local district's white shield with the words "Here lies Angelika 1980–2006," everything in me bristled; I saw and did not know if I wanted to see.

The words "here lies" were wrong. I do not believe that even one person in the whole cemetery really rests there. "In memory of" or "in remembrance of" would be more fitting. But what does it matter, it doesn't change the fact of her death. We stood at the grave for a long time in silence. I couldn't believe it. It hurts so much. Over and over again I read the white plaque with "Here lies Angelika 1980–2006." As if it might change? As if I could not believe it, even after reading it for the twentieth time. Each time I felt like I was seeing it for the first time.

Leaves blew from the tree onto her grave, the sun warmed us despite the cold November air.

I could not say anything. Just cry and sob. As though I would never stop, as though my life now consisted only of sobs. At some point I could barely stand anymore. So I knelt down by the grave. Just knelt like that sobbing by the rose bush. I cleared the leaves from the grave, placed the postcard of Bryce Canyon and the little pink flower on it, and wept. I have no idea how long I was kneeling at the grave. Andi also stood in front of the grave and cried. But in those moments I could not bear even his touch. Nothing could comfort me.

Why did you leave me? Why couldn't you see all the love? Why didn't you seek help? Why didn't you say anything?

So I knelt there, cried, and the thoughts raced through my head. At some point Angelika's favorite psalm came to mind. Psalm 63: "God, you are my God, I seek you, my soul thirsts for you; My flesh faints for you, as in a dry and weary land where there is no water."[1] I quietly spoke the psalm to myself. As I said it I thought, "Angelika is not thirsty anymore, her favorite psalm is fulfilled, she is with God and her thirst has been quenched. Nothing and no one can change that now or take her away from the presence of God." So I sat there, praying, crying out, and sobbing to God. Gradually my tears ran dry, gradually I was able to calm down somewhat, and my breathing became calmer. God was near, yes, somehow there. And yet, Angelika, I miss you so much, there is not one second except in sleep when I am not missing you and thinking of you. I feel as though, since your death, I belong neither among the living nor the dead. I am somewhere in a world in between, and cannot participate in life, nor in death.

I can barely laugh with others, have no share in life, and hardly ever see people. I live and feel dead inside. All I can do is sit and cry. I do not want to accept life or death. What else is left?

Standing at the grave and seeing the tombstone with my deceased friend's name on it was a shock. Now the whole reality of her death had caught up with me. Now there was no more secretly wishing that she was still alive. Only when the loved one's death becomes real do further steps on the path of mourning become possible.

The confrontation with reality strangled me initially; I was inconsolable and could not move from the graveside. Until Psalm 63 came to mind. There is a power in learning to grieve with biblical experiences. These millennia-old texts, containing the grieving experiences of entire generations, can serve as signposts on the complex and involuntary path of mourning. They can become companions who bring language to speechlessness and hope to

1. All translations of the Bible are from the NRSV.

despair, and thereby provide comfort. There are many biblical texts that can serve this purpose. A few especially helpful ones are the Psalms (e.g., Pss 23, 63, 121, 139), Ecclesiastes, or Job in the Old Testament; or from the New Testament, the calming of the storm (Mark 4:35–41), the story of the road to Emmaus (Luke 24:13–39), or the everlasting love of God (Rom 8:38–39).

The Lonely Paths of Grief

The paths of grief are paths that one must, in part, travel alone. It is natural to feel lonely in such situations. But after a suicide, survivors often experience a profound isolation and alienation from their environment, which goes beyond the normal level of being alone.

10. COMMUNITY—THAT IS NOT SUPPORTIVE

After the "crash landing," every task and activity lost its meaning, and even people, with their lightheartedness and lack of worries, became alien to me. Jokes and small talk were hardly bearable. I did not understand much anymore, did not have the energy to engage in what is supposedly "superficial." I found my emotional state at that time expressed most aptly in Hermann Hesse's poem "In the Fog":[1]

> In the Fog
> Strange, to wander in the fog.
> Each bush and stone stands alone,
> No tree sees the next one,
> Each is alone.
>
> My world was full of friends
> When my life was filled with light,

1. Source of the translation: Horton, "Hesse's 'In the Fog.'"

Now as the fog descends
None is still to be seen.

Truly there is no wise man
Who does not know the dark
Which quietly and inescapably
Separates him from everything else.

Strange, to wander in the fog,
To live is to be alone.
No man knows the next man,
Each is alone.

"Now as the fog descends, none is still to be seen."
I no longer saw anyone and was somehow also unseen.
Perhaps my heaviness, my lack of understanding for nor-
mality pushed people away? Before my honeymoon and
above all before Angelika's death I was very engaged
and involved in the church, but after my return there
was simply nothing left. Six months earlier, 340 people
had come to our wedding, many of them from my youth
work and the church. But now no one was there. I had
invested in many people, supported, coached, and encouraged them. But now that I needed comfort, encour-
agement, and friendship, "none was to be seen." My
roommate, my longtime coach, and my partner—they
were there, unobtrusive, patient, helpless; but they
were not afraid. And later my church mentor became
important as well. Likewise, my personal faith remained
with me. Even though this consisted primarily of cries of
anger, accusations, and doubts about God, I still had an
anchor to provide some stability. I stubbornly held on to
the hope for hope.

But where were my many former friends from the
church and youth work? Alongside my grief and despair
came a deep disappointment with the "church" or at
least with what I had understood "church" to mean up
to that point. For me, the church had become a pious

bunch of sanctimonious people who are only there when everything looks good, when you are doing well. But in the fog, there was no one left. Hesse's words became experienced and lived reality: "To live is to be alone." How could that be? I wrote in my diary,

> What is church? I don't know anymore. Not even what I believe in. The things that seemed so clear and unshakable have turned out to be illusions. . . . I have no idea what church is anymore. I don't believe in an institution, in methods, in "secularization" or "Christianization." The body of Christ (the church) must be something other than what I know. What could it be?

After Angelika's suicide, my social contacts were massively reduced. I lived in a parallel world and contact with other people was difficult. I could only participate in their questions, in laughter, and in "normalcy" with great effort. That was certainly strange and new for many people. I was actually known for taking the initiative and reaching out to people.

In this difficult period of mourning it became clear that the people in my life had relied on my taking the initiative. And so almost no one reached out to me. It probably would have been helpful if people had made an effort to help me, especially in this situation. If they had not been afraid to meet me. If they had invited me out, visited me, or taken me with them somewhere. I'm sure I was difficult to endure with my grief and despair, but encounters with others can bring comfort. I would not have needed many words, nor any well-meaning advice or wisdom. Encounters and relationships with others were helpful when people were not afraid of me and my grief, where they supported me together with everything that entailed.

In comparison with people left behind by other kinds of death, those affected by suicide experience less support and are judged more negatively socially. At the same time, they withdraw more from the world and demand less social support for themselves.[2] The result is that loneliness and isolation are further reinforced.[3]

The first part of the story of Job reveals how friends can be supportive in silence and empathy (Job 2:11–13). I know of no other story that so aptly illustrates this. Job sat in dust and ashes, inconsolable, grieving, and hurt. He didn't say a word. His friends

2. Wagner, *Komplizierte Trauer*, 20 and 48–49.
3. Wagner, *Komplizierte Trauer*, 49.

sat with him and remained silent for seven days and nights (in biblical terms: as long as it was necessary). Their silent presence comforted Job and gradually allowed him to speak, albeit with bitter, searching, and questioning words. Their silent presence released Job from his internal, silent numbness.

Silent care, especially in the first period of mourning, cannot simply relieve the feeling of deep loneliness. But comfort can be given through friendship and in the encounter with another person.[4] Well-meaning tips and recommendations to see life in a positive light, or people who try to persuade someone that there is a "greater meaning" behind a suicide, or consolations such as "you will see her again in heaven" are not helpful. These remarks only reinforce loneliness and isolation. Social contacts in which the bereaved are spoken to, perceived, and seen[5] are supportive encounters.

4. Sometimes helplessness itself can be helpful. Schibilsky, *Trauerwege*, 34.

5. Buber, *Das dialogische Prinzip*, 10.

Inner Life in the Mourning Process

Grief is not a linear process—especially in the case of suicide. One's inner life sometimes resembles an emotional chaos in which even in internal dialogues the addressee becomes confused. Thoughts turn in circles and feelings alternate among self-doubt, guilt, and resignation.

> ## 11. FROM MY DIARY (OCTOBER 29, 2006)
>
> It hurts so much that Angelika is not here anymore. Everything reminds me of her, my day is filled with memories and thoughts of her. No matter where I look, my gaze always returns to our friendship. I just want to scream all day, call out to you, undo the whole thing. Yes, my life is full of memories, full of your life, and you're not here anymore, you're gone, of your own accord, without saying goodbye.
>
> How can my life be full of your life, even though you're dead? Why? Again and again I ask this question. I would so love to sit here with you, drink a coffee, talk, laugh, or just hug you.
>
> I know that I will never again have the kind of friendship we had.

You've gone, left me behind. I have to live with this fact. Yes, you heard right, I have to live with it and some day, when my God-given time comes, I also have to die with it. But I will be happy to see you again, to have time with you that we no longer have here on earth.

But even this anticipation doesn't help me overcome my pain and loneliness.

Oh, if you were only here, I have so many ideas. . . . Now they fly away in the autumn wind. They don't have a person where they can land, where they can dream.

Why did you throw everything away? Even our friendship?

I feel alone, so alone, and I long for you. For your laugh and your sensitive manner, for the hours of conversation with you, studying together, I long for our sarcastic conversations.

You're gone. I just have to accept it, can't do anything about it. Our friendship was so important to me, you were so important to me. Why?

I hope you are safe, comforted in the arms of God. I hope all your tears have been wiped away and you can live and love without pain.

Even if our friendship could not keep you here, if the longing for death, maybe also for the kingdom of God, was greater than the will to live, I hope with my whole heart that I was able to show you in our friendship how loved and treasured you are.

I can't do anything but cry—and even that doesn't seem to be enough, I have to suppress my screams, though they would express my pain much better. How else can I vent my sadness and make the pain bearable? I don't know and I can't do it. I feel inconsolable and desperate.

God, life goes on and I seem to stand still. It has already been two and a half months since the suicide, two and a half months and I feel like it's only been a few days. I don't feel like you've already been gone for two and a half months. No, it just happened. Sometimes I still feel like I can reach out to you. You are still here, you are still so present in my daily life, I am waiting to finally be able to see you, but we won't see each other again here on earth. In my head I know that, I know you are gone . . . but I can't, I don't want to.

A candle is burning on the table, it's already getting dark, though it's only 6:15. I am alone, still, I hoped that Andi or Andrea would come home soon. But no one is here and it is quiet—very quiet. But this candle is burning here, bright. Christ is the light that shines in the darkness, and no darkness can extinguish it. So, with these eyes I look at candles again and again. With the certainty of the light of God that shines and is able to give warmth even in deepest pain and in despair.

The light doesn't take away my pain, doesn't silence my crying and my internal screaming (not yet, not now), but it burns with the full power of hope. What can I hope for, except for you, my God?

I wanted to leave this diary entry as it was. My internal conflict, the battle with reality, the pain and denial are expressed in it. This is reflected, for example, in the language. There is a change from one sentence to the next. Sometimes I speak directly to Angelika, then the words are addressed to no one and in the next sentence God becomes the conversation partner. It felt as though the emotions and thoughts were riding on a carousel that was turning far too quickly. One feeling was followed by the next thought. Faith was followed by doubt, longing, and despair. But again and again, the unbelievable pain over my loss and the lost dreams stood in the foreground.

Those left behind by suicide have to cope not only with the pain of loss, but also with the feeling of having been existentially rejected and rebuffed. The friendship, all the plans and hopes were freely, willingly rejected (at least to the extent that a suicide is in fact a free choice). Thus many mourners are left with a feeling of deep abandonment and rejection.

Follow-Up Care as Prevention

After a suicide, life can become unbearable for those left behind. Especially within close circles of family and friends of the deceased, suicides are often followed by further suicides. The urgency and importance of follow-up care should therefore not be underestimated.

---

12. YEARNING FOR DEATH

Life and death seek one another, define one another.
Dancing in the game of the tides,
wrestling over passing away or being.
Hope, self-confident, steps forward, and then back again.
Carried away by the wind,
blown by the wings of the storm.
What remains are questions, seeking and straying,
dead ends and bridges,
Yearning for infinity.

Angelika's death not only left a gaping wound in me, but called my own life into question, as I tried to describe at the time in the above poem. I had no answer to the question of how I should exist without Angelika. Over and over again I lost myself in grief and despair to the point that I myself no longer wanted to live. I was lost, and felt drawn sometimes to life, sometimes to death, driven hither and thither by the wind. My longing

---

for my friend grew and with it the longing to be dead myself. But no one could, no one must know that except for my diary, to which I entrusted the following just after the new year on January 2, 2007:

> Today I am not bearable for anyone. I just want to disappear, dissolve in the air and no longer exist. No longer breathe, no longer live, no longer endure. Be gone in order to be no more. I cannot take it anymore, I can't, I can't do it anymore. I long for a paradise, a place without pain, or just to be non-existent. Everything is difficult for me, sleep is closer to me than life. I constantly want to flee from a waking state, so that I don't have to endure being awake and my grief. I feel powerless against this apathy towards life.

I struggled with myself and my life in silence and in secret. No one was allowed to know, no one spoke to me about it. On the one hand I experienced with my own body how painful, difficult, and overwhelming the suicide of a loved one can be. I could not, must not do that to anyone. I did not want to put my partner and the people I trusted in the same situation I found myself in.

And yet. . . . My longing for death was there. I could not ignore it, I could not talk myself out of it or downplay it.

But what made my suicidal thoughts even stronger were those damned feelings of guilt. Grief threatened to suffocate me again and again, but the feelings of guilt made me aggressive—against myself. I hated myself for the fact that Angelika had taken her own life.

Again and again I asked myself what I could have done to prevent her death. I was convinced that I had failed as a friend and that's why she was dead now. Living with these feelings of guilt was difficult, almost unbearable. And so I lived day by day with the desire to be dead. Quiet on the outside and wrestling with myself

> internally, because I did not want to put my partner and friends in the same situation of grief that I was experiencing myself. But: if I were dead, everything would be so simple, nothing would matter to me then. I would be home, where my friend is.

There is good reason that it is repeatedly pointed out that the risk of suicide can increase considerably for the close friends and relatives left behind by a suicide.

Much of one's previous life is called into question through the loss, so that the life of those in mourning can suddenly lose its own meaning. Why should they still exist when a part of their life is missing and guilt, shame, stigmatization, isolation, and a deep feeling of abandonment are piled on top of the loss of meaning? Thus, for some survivors, life becomes unbearable and they, too, come to regard suicide as a reasonable way out of this psychological emergency situation. In comparison with the general population, the risk of suicide among the bereaved is between two and ten times greater.[1] There are studies showing that among adolescents who are grieving a suicide the risk of taking their own life is five times greater than among adolescents who are grieving due to another cause of death.[2]

Due to the fact that many funerals still take place within one of the regional churches, at least the pastor and sometimes also church volunteers are aware of who has been left behind by a suicide. Here, pastoral outreach that seeks integration instead of isolation and speaking up instead of silence can have a connecting and comforting impact. And it can do so in such a way that the solace of the gospel can not only be heard, but experienced: "And the light shines in the darkness, and the darkness did not overcome it" (John 1:5). The potential of a supportive Christian community in the processing of a suicide should not be underestimated. At the same time, it can make an important contribution to suicide prevention. Beyond this, follow-up care requires not only local pastoral caregivers, but also regional points of contact (within the church) that can support and connect survivors. Self-help groups have also proved to be helpful in dealing with a suicide.[3]

1. Runeson and Åsberg, "Family History of Suicide," 1525–26.

2. Aguirre and Slater, "Suicide Postvention as Suicide Prevention," 530–31.

3. Specifically for fifteen- to thirty-year-old survivors, for example, Nebelmeer is a good, safe starting point in Zurich, Bern, and Biel: www.nebelmeer. net. For further information, see the chapter titled "Specialist Agencies and Support Services."

Daily Life Is a Minefield

After every death, the life of those left behind is full of objects and places that remind them of the person they have lost: the deceased is everywhere. For some people this is comforting. But in the case of a suicide, these very memories can also be distressing, since one is confronted everywhere not just with the deceased, but also with one's own feelings of guilt, anger, despair, and fear.

13. NOT-PLACES AND SAFE SPACES

As indicated in entry #8, "Crash Landing," it was no longer possible for me to continue my studies after Angelika's suicide. My life made no sense anymore, why should my studies still be important?

Even more unbearable for me than the meaninglessness was the fact that "our" studies and "our" plans should become "my" studies and "my" plans. Neither reason nor discipline brought me to the point of getting on the train and going to Zurich to the Faculty of Theology. My fear of being overwhelmed by the memories and being unable to endure the pain was too great. We had studied together for more than four years, so every corner of the faculty building was filled with memories. In the "Sternchensaal" we had made it through Hebrew and blew into the shofar, in room 108 we had translated parts of the New Testament and Greek philosophers, and with glasses full of wine in the foyer had tried to understand Descartes, Augustine, and Leibniz. In every nook and cranny we had studied, eaten, and drunk coffee together, and hardly a day went by in the faculty without a tournament at the foosball table. Over the years we had become an almost invincible team. With Angelika on offense and me on defense, we won many victories. Our roles in foosball were exactly the opposite of the rest of our lives.

All this and more flooded my mind instantly whenever I thought of going to Zurich. Intuitively, I knew that I would probably fall apart at the latest at the top floor of the Faculty of Theology, by the foosball table in the foyer. I actually still was owed a secret wedding gift from Angelika—there was supposed to be a foosball table waiting for us after our honeymoon. But it never came to that. The foosball table became the embodiment of unfulfilled wishes and promises and the symbol of our friendship, broken by suicide. What I did not yet know at that time: I would not touch a foosball table for many years to come—I avoided this game "like the devil avoids holy water."

I avoided any and all reminders of our studies—yet I could not escape the reminders in my everyday life, the temporal and emotional emptiness that this friendship left behind. When I was not sitting paralyzed somewhere or working, I made an effort to remove from my sight everything that could somehow remind me of Angelika. Once I accidentally came across a photo of my friend. I stared at the picture as if struck by lightning and froze. From that point on I tried to avoid pictures, objects, and even the name of my friend. The reminders had to go— as if they had never existed.

After someone has been lost, places, smells, objects, and activities suddenly become loaded with emotion and significance. A living place, like the university, can become desolate, "non-places." Activities like studying, drinking coffee, and playing a foosball tournament can become a minefield of overwhelming memories. That's how it was with me. After the suicide, many things were so strongly connected with Angelika that it was no longer possible for me to do certain activities or be in certain places. I felt as though I was drowning in memories and the more connected they were with physical spaces, smells, or activities, the higher the water rose.

For the "outside world," this behavior is difficult to understand, but those who are grieving know such places that trigger their memories. It is not wrong to avoid these places in the first few months for the sake of relief. The struggle with the reality of the suicide, with grief, loss, anger, guilt, love, and hate already takes up enough space. However, one must distinguish between avoidance behavior that has a stabilizing impact, and behavior that takes on pathological features.[1]

When familiar places become "non-places," it can be helpful to create new safe spaces and explore new areas. It takes large reserves of psychological strength before one can return to such minefields. This strength can be found in a small, safe, newly developed space of one's life. What this space looks like and where it is located must be discovered independently by the person who is grieving. Some people create an internal retreat, others go to a church, sit under a tree, or go on a journey. I personally found this place at a farm.

1. See the chapter titled "Theory of Grief." For the diagnosis of complicated grief, cf., e.g., Wagner, *Komplizierte Trauer*, 14–16.

Physical Activity as Grief Counselor

Grief has not just psychological but also physical aspects. These include, for example, sleep disorders, respiratory, cardiac, or digestive complaints, disorders of the immune system, loss of appetite, or increased mortality. The whole body is thus required on the path of grief. The body is often a neglected part of the mourning process. Intense emotions can be regulated via the body. In addition, the body can bring about empowerment for those in mourning. In the face of emotional and cognitive feelings of powerlessness, one can make one's way back to a capacity for action through physical activity.

14. FROM THE UNIVERSITY TO THE COWSHED

Since the university and my theological studies became non-places, it was impossible for me to resume my studies after Angelika's suicide. I returned to my job as a teacher, but only at 40 percent—the other 60 percent of my time that was meant for my studies was left empty and unfulfilled. At that time we had been back in Switzerland for six weeks, and I knew intuitively that I must not simply sit at home, as I faced a daily deluge of despair. Since I had shared a flat with a trained farmer for a long time, the idea of going to work at a farm gradually grew. I loved animals, I was small and thin but never hesitated to do physical work, and I enjoyed being outdoors. So I contacted a farmer I knew and offered my help. He was happy to accept my offer and so I began to work three or four days a week at the farm. I dove into an entirely different world. I washed potatoes, swept out the barn, collected garbage in the pastures, packed meat and eggs, cut trees, knocked down walls, rebuilt the attic, and chopped wood. Every day at lunch I emptied the big pots of food together with the family. This kind of work makes you hungry! My appetite returned and anyone who works ten hours a day on a farm sleeps better at night. The work on the farm was rigorous, but very good for me. I especially enjoyed breaking down tree trunks into firewood. Sometimes I worked until I had let all my anger out. And so there were times when I had carried and broken down more than three tons of wood by the evening. I became acquainted with the healing effects of chopping wood and physical labor. My anger and grief found an outlet when I worked alone in the field or in the forest. Our existential dependence on nature, which became clear to me on the farm, did me good. You can only sow seed where you have plowed, and can only harvest what you have cultivated. Much of what I ate and drank on the farm was produced right there, it was the fruit of the labor that I was a part of. We had made the juice we drank, the meat that we packed came from the cattle on the farm (even if I did not eat it), etc. Life and death seemed closer on the farm, more natural, and so Angelika's suicide lost at least a little bit of its unnatural nature.

Especially when one is so directly affected by a suicide and stuck in the midst of grief, it is difficult to do anything at all or to get excited about something. In the first few weeks I sat alone at home a lot and sank into my grief. But reason told me that this could not be a long-term solution. I do not know where I got the strength to look for work on a farm. But it was a good decision. I didn't earn anything, but I learned a lot. Working on the farm forced me out of my isolation and I was now with people every day. Physical labor was good for me psychologically and physically.[1] I learned how essential it can be to work together, when, for example, renovating an attic or felling a tree. I learned that our human body can achieve much more than I had thought. I was not always put to work in the farmyard, I was often not doing well, but that was okay. I worked and so did the others. We ate together and let ourselves live—without too many expectations. Certainly working on a farm is not the best option for all mourners to begin to make their way back to life. But perhaps there are other meaningful activities? Working with an animal shelter? Social and/or physical activities? Exercise and physical activity not only helps with depression, but can also awaken new "spirits" in the long process of mourning, and can transform anger and grief.

1. Seidler et.al, *Handbuch der Psychotraumatologie*, 238.

Holidays as Particular Challenges

Holidays are especially challenging not only for many people without family but also for those in mourning. Christmas is probably the most difficult holiday because especially during this time many survivors feel that they have to force themselves to function and be happy.

15. HOW DO YOU CELEBRATE CHRISTMAS?

Although I dragged myself through each day, life inexorably continued, at least on the calendar: October, November, December. Christmas was getting closer and closer and I was growing farther and farther from people. Very few concrete memories from this period have remained; instead, I have impressions of dull, foggy feelings, disorientation, and strangeness. I did not notice the Christmas lights on the streets, houses, and shopping centers. But when I came near a store, I heard the familiar Christmas music. "Jingle Bells" and "Last Christmas" droned around me and the shop windows were full of glittering, unnecessary things. People streamed through the streets and everyone was preparing for the holidays. These Christmas preparations passed before my eyes like a strange, distorted film. Celebrate? What could I celebrate? The dark winter? The gray days? A holiday without my friend? But I was occupied less by the question of the "what" than the "how": how could I celebrate, now that nothing was as it should be?

I dreaded Christmas, the family celebrations, the apparently happy faces. But even more than that, I found the theologically loaded stories repugnant: Mary and Joseph, the donkey, Bethlehem and the three kings, a God who became human. I didn't want a God who became human, a celebration, opulent meals and lights; no, I wanted Angelika back. That was my only wish.

Christmas and Boxing Day were in fact very difficult. It was exhausting to maintain a reasonably cheerful facade, to hold trivial conversations, and not show that anything was wrong. I did not want to ruin anyone's holiday and, socially speaking, people in mourning are not necessarily the most pleasant. For everyone else, Angelika was already long since dead. She was not family, she was just a friend, an acquaintance, whom most people did not know well. I played along. Only once did I lose my composure, when my grandmother mentioned my late friend and I sensed her bewilderment at the suicide. As described in the first sections of this book, hardly anyone said Angelika's name aloud. Except my grandmother. Even years later, she did not forget about the suicide and lamented what was, in her worldview, a "squandered" life.

Holidays are considered to be particular challenges for those in mourning, and all the more so for survivors of a suicide. On the one hand, the absence of the deceased is particularly noticeable in these times; on the other hand, the pressure to function normally is even greater. This causes those in mourning to feel lonely and misunderstood, or to withdraw and isolate themselves. At Christmas, the holiday in which God became human, it would be appropriate for us to also become human for those left behind by a suicide. Specifically, it would be a relief if mourners could participate in the holiday without having to maintain facades, if joy and sorrow were given equal space. The holidays are also filled with family rituals and commitments. Sometimes it is necessary for those in mourning to listen to themselves and to consider which people and forms of celebration are beneficial. This can also mean breaking family traditions and creating new holiday rituals.

Mourning as an Encounter with the Void

The inner life of those left behind after a suicide is difficult to understand for people on the outside. What used to bring a person joy no longer matters to them. What they used to do often, they no longer do, because the person in mourning is confronted again and again with the paralyzing emptiness.

16. BLANK SPACES

Christmas was over and the new year was about to begin. For the first time in ten years, I did not want to go to the church's New Year's camp. Normally I loved the New Year's camp, I knew almost all of the more than one hundred participants, and before Angelika's death I had been a constant part of this Christian community.

But a lot had changed since Angelika's death. I no longer felt like a part of this community. Large crowds of people horrified me. I felt even lonelier among people and became even more painfully aware of the hole that Angelika had left behind. I did not feel understood by the people from my church, but rather alienated. In addition, all the hymns and worship songs were a farce for me. How could I sing "Great God, We Praise You" or "Shine, Jesus, Shine," when I felt completely different?

No, all these songs would no longer cross my lips. They were not a comfort, but had mutated into pure provocations in my life.

So I stayed home; I did not want to celebrate the transition from 2006 to 2007, did not want to see any people, did not want to have to put on the cheerful "Christmas mask" again. I also did not know what I would have to celebrate, since only this emptiness remained in me. The loss of Angelika was the only thing I could still see, the only thing that mattered. Everything else in my life became completely meaningless. Even the people who were kind to me, who tried to understand me, like my husband and my longtime friend and roommate, I no longer truly perceived. They were unable to get through to me.

The empty space that Angelika had left in my life surrounded me like a chasm. It was quiet all around me and all of life was swallowed up by this vast emptiness. I was incapable of bridging this seemingly insurmountable pit.

I would have so loved to share more life with Angelika. In my diary I lamented the stolen time:

> I would have wished for more time, more conversations, more experiences with you. Wouldn't you have wished for more? Angelika, why did you leave me alone, a voice inside me screams over and over again.

She cheated me and us out of our shared dreams, our shared time, and as I perceived it only a nothingness remained.

As my example shows, those left behind by a suicide can become overwhelmed by the feeling of emptiness. The emptiness is symptomatic of the complicated grief experienced by many survivors of a suicide.[1] Life, friendships, beloved people—I could no longer see the beauty in any of it. After a suicide, one mourns not only for the person themselves, but also for the lost time and shattered dreams. More so than with other causes of death, a suicide leaves the feeling that the deceased intentionally destroyed shared dreams and robbed survivors of their time together. This emptiness sometimes destroys many bridges connecting a survivor to the world. Bridges to tasks, activities, and people that were previously cherished. In this emptiness, songs that used to be comforting and familiar texts can elicit anger and rejection. As previously described (see "Grieving with Biblical Experiences"), biblical texts and traditional prayers can support the mourning process. However, liturgical forms—which I also consider to include worship songs—also harbor the risk that they might have an alienating or cynical impact in grief. The contents of familiar prayers and songs can run contrary to the internal experience of those left behind and thus increase feelings of emptiness, loneliness, and hopelessness. Which texts and songs are comforting and which are provoking or even hurtful depends entirely on each individual. But in the positive case, especially in the context of pastoral support, they can foster a cognitive understanding of one's own mechanisms of grief.

The emptiness also destroyed bridges to other people. At that point, I was unable to rebuild these bridges. As has often been mentioned, other people who make an effort to fill the days of those in grief with life and do not shrink from their sometimes hostile manner are crucial to progress in the process of mourning. It is essential to accept the grief and emptiness of those left behind. But it is just as important to build small bridges of hope towards the person in mourning. A brief visit, a slice of cake, a kind word, a card, a smile, an activity, a sign of friendship, a glass of wine together, a study group, a phone call, a hug, an open ear, a link for a specialist, paints and paper, coffee, and much more. . . . It does not take much to begin building a bridge, just a bit of courage, but every building block can have a significant impact.

1. See the chapter titled "Theory of Grief."

Avoidance Behavior
on the Path of Grief

On some paths of grief there are also "restricted areas." These can be mental, physical, visual, or personal. One must first recognize these restricted zones and become aware of them in order for movement back into everyday life to be possible. Grief counselors and spiritual advisors can play an important role in this.

> ## 17. BACK TO DAILY LIFE (1):
> ## RECOGNIZING RESTRICTED AREAS
>
> Spring was already approaching; the days were getting longer and a bit warmer. But I had not returned to my studies. I could not and did not want to study, but above all I still did not feel capable of going to Zurich. Even before my honeymoon and before Angelika's suicide, I had arranged a meeting with my church mentor for the spring of 2007. Since I do not like to cancel appointments, I went to the meeting. In my pastoral education program, every person who intended to complete the practical training as a pastor following their studies was required to have a pastor as a mentor. The task of this mentor was to support the student during their studies and to attend the obligatory aptitude tests for ecclesial

service. When I met my mentor in the parish hall, he did not know that I was no longer studying. I had known him for a few years now and found him to be competent and trustworthy. So I told him about my friend's suicide and my feeling of being lost. I hesitantly continued and explained that I had not returned to my studies and that I did not know if I would ever be able to do so. Although I was embarrassed, I told him about this invisible, insurmountable wall, which seemed to stand between Zurich Oberland and the city of Zurich, and which made it impossible for me to go back to university. My mentor listened attentively and asked a few questions. He wanted to know if I was afraid of the city of Zurich in general or if there were certain areas that were causing me trouble. He asked about the places where we had studied together and wanted to know which rooms in the university I was particularly afraid of. He asked where I had met Angelika and where we had spent the most time together. My mentor approached the topic gradually. Through his targeted questions, he forced me to become more specific, to identify my fear, and to assign memories to particular places and rooms. We began, like cartographers, to survey the area and mark boundaries and landmarks. This gave shape to my fear and it became more tangible. I thus realized that I was not afraid of Zurich itself, but of the area around the Faculty of Theology. My anxiety rose as I approached the Faculty of Theology in my mind. Most of all, I was afraid of the lounge, where I had met Angelika. Where we had cooked, studied, and played foosball together.

I was able to establish that my fear grew linearly according to the amount of memories that I ascribed to certain rooms and spaces. The more memories with Angelika that I could associate with a place, the greater my fear of this space. My fear became more concrete, was given a shape and an outline. It was the fear that I would be so overwhelmed by grief over my loss that I would not be able to bear it any longer. I was afraid of not being able to absorb and channel these feelings, and of being entirely alone in these places laden with memories.

Toward the end of the conversation my mentor paused, thought for a moment, and suggested that we go to Zurich and visit these places together. I knew that he was an experienced emergency counselor, who also trained people in emergency counseling. So I agreed to his suggestion and we agreed on an appointment for the following week.

People who suffer from complicated grief demonstrate increased avoidance behavior. Like those with post-traumatic stress disorder, they avoid memories and places because intrusions and unbearable reactions of grief might arise. In addition, avoidance behavior leads those in mourning to withdraw from people and activities that would actually support their grieving process.[1]

It was a stroke of luck that I had a highly qualified pastor who was very experienced in emergency counseling as my mentor. He recognized that my fear hovered over me like a dark cloud. By helping me to identify the fear and to ascribe my memories to specific places and spaces, it lost its overwhelming power and became tangible. With his help it became possible to look my fear in the face, or in the geographical places, spaces, and memories. It is often impossible to reduce such fears on one's own; rather, it is necessary for a competent pastor or specialist to help in this task. Breaking through the structures of fear requires targeted exposure. It is essential that someone be familiar with the issue, be capable of conducting a pastoral counseling session adapted to the circumstances, and potentially be able to take charge of the situation. Specialists, pastors, competent supporters, and advisors are central in this step of coping with grief. They are the ones who can

1. Wagner, *Komplizierte Trauer*, 16–19.

point toward paths that are passable, and can walk them together with the grieving person. People in mourning with avoidance behaviors have neither the ability to see nor the emotional capacity to walk this path alone. It requires helpers and specialists who build bridges back to life and to daily routine.

Supported Exposure and Restricted Areas

In order to overcome avoidance behavior, various forms of exposure are needed. In addition to the conscious, emotional, and mental confrontation with memories and activities being avoided, a visit to difficult places can have positive effects on the continued mourning process.

18. BACK TO DAILY LIFE (2): ENTERING RESTRICTED AREAS

I somewhat hesitantly agreed to my mentor's suggestion of going together with him to Zurich to the Faculty of Theology. It reassured me to know that he had often visited places that had become internal restricted areas with those left behind by a suicide.

We discussed in advance which places we would visit and we agreed on a timeframe. My mentor explained in detail how he organized such "visits." He explained that we would take several breaks and spend time at the individual places. That he would want to know in each case how I was doing and would also ask about specific memories. There was one week between the first conversation and the planned visit to the restricted areas. During this week I repeatedly regretted having agreed to this. I doubted the idea of it, was happy to hide away with my fear, and certainly did not want to be confronted with it. But fortunately, my pride and stubbornness stopped me from canceling the appointment with my mentor. In addition, his calm and competent nature had convinced me and I trusted him to have the situation under control.

So we met a week later at 10:00 a.m. at the train station in Wetzikon and took the S5 toward Zurich Stadelhofen. In the train we initially talked about trivial matters, then he again explained the plan for the visit.

We planned to walk from Stadelhofen train station to the Faculty of Theology at Grossmünster. There we wanted to visit certain places and spaces and to spend more time in the lounge—the most difficult place for me. The visit would end at Florhofgasse, where the Practical Theology department was located at the time. Fortunately it was a sunny day, so we got off the train at the Stadelhofen station and sat down on a bench first. I was nauseated from nervousness, fear, or for whatever reason. But as we sat on the bench and I showed my mentor where Angelika and I had always met, it got better, I became calmer. The train station was suddenly no longer terrifying; instead, it again became a lively space with lots of coming and going. After a few minutes, we got up and walked to the Faculty of Theology. On the way there, my mentor wanted to know a bit more about what my friendship with Angelika was like, what united us, what we had experienced together outside of university life. I told him about our time sharing a flat, the nightly jogs up Bachtel mountain, and the highs and lows of our friendship. We also talked about Angelika's psychological problems, her negative self-image, and my constant fear of a suicide. When we arrived at the faculty, we first went into the room where I had met Angelika in our Hebrew class. In this room I told my mentor about the beginnings of our friendship. I described to him how I noticed this shy and amiable person and asked her if she wanted to study together. It was probably the first time since Angelika's suicide that these memories did not just make me sad, but I was also able to find a little joy in them. Together we continued into other seminar rooms, into the library, the second floor, and then to the third floor until we stood in the lounge. Everything appeared to be the same as before. The chairs, the mess around the sink, the refrigerator, and a little farther back the foosball table. At the sight of the foosball table, I went numb inside. We had loved this thing so much. We had been a great team, almost unbeatable. My mentor and I sat down. Haltingly, I told him about this place and my many memories here. It was strange to sit there; the room looked exactly the same and yet everything felt different. After a long time we made our way to the last stage of our visit, the Flo-rhofgasse. But after I had "survived" the lounge, this last station was no longer a problem.

It was an intense morning; many memories and emotions had been shaken to the surface. But it had been worth it. I knew that I would be capable of taking up my studies again. After more than two hours we returned to the train station, where we looked back on the visit and then went our separate ways.

Not all those who are grieving protect themselves from their memories and emotions with restricted areas that are geographic. Others, for example, create restricted areas by stopping certain activities or no longer looking at objects that are laden with memories. Approaching these restricted areas, whether they are objects or places, is an important step in the mourning process. In complicated grief, various forms of exposure have a positive effect on the process of mourning.[1] It is an action that leads back to life. Those who are accompanied in these steps by a competent and sensitive support person or specialist are not only able to overcome avoidance behavior, but simultaneously break out of their emotional isolation. Since support persons are not trapped by fear and grief and will not be overwhelmed by personal emotions, they can maintain an external perspective on the situation (or the location) and at the same time be aware of the internal state of the grieving person. Being "under control" here means empathetically bringing together the threads of emotions, memories, places, activities, and

1. Wittouck et al., "Prevention and Treatment of Complicated Grief," 69–78.

objects without overloading the grieving person. If this succeeds, fears can be dismantled and restricted areas can once again become places of life.

Liberating Rage

For many of those left behind, if not all, at some point after a suicide emotions such as anger and outrage emerge. Many are angry with the deceased person for leaving them. Anger can also be directed against one's social environment, the therapist of the person who committed suicide, or their family. Although anger is evaluated negatively in our society, one's own life can gradually return through these very emotions.

19. ANGER BREAKS THROUGH

Eight months after Angelika's suicide, I had dared to go back to the university for the first time. I had entered the restricted area and invisible barriers had collapsed. But this first visit did not pass by without a leaving a mark. The next day, a whirlwind of memory and emotion raged within me. Until then, Angelika's suicide had often left me in a paralyzing numbness, despair, and seemingly endless grief. But now other emotions came to the fore, emotions that were already there but that I had not yet consciously been aware of. I wrote the following in my diary:

> Yesterday I was back in Zurich at the faculty building the first time, thanks to Peter. But I felt so lonely and abandoned without Angelika. Everything seemed to me so familiar and at the same time foreign. I once

again became painfully aware of how much I feel alone and forsaken by Angelika. Nothing mattered anymore, the plans, agreements, but most of all our friendship—everything became so meaningless to her that she just threw it away. Sometimes, faced with Angelika's death, I feel like I will never be able to really laugh again, I am either deeply sad or unbelievably angry.

Anger and disappointment mingled now more and more with the feelings of grief and loneliness. She had thrown it all away, all our shared plans, arrangements, promises, everything. How could she do that to me, to us? It was not fair, damn it! I was seething with anger and deeply disappointed in Angelika. At the same time I was shocked by my strong emotions. Was I allowed to be so angry at my friend? Was that legitimate? She could not help herself—could she? I paced the living room like a tiger in a cage. I did not know what to do with my anger. Should I let it out against myself? My roommates? I could have screamed with disappointment—but I stayed silent. Initially. At some point I put on my running shoes and jogged into the closest woods. I stood there alone, stomped my feet and kicked all the trees around me. Again and again I hit and kicked the tree trunks. I was unbelievably angry with my dead friend and no longer had a target at which to direct my anger, Angelika had escaped everything and I was left alone with my anger and accusations. Eventually I was tired out from hitting and kicking and already had bruises on my arms and legs—but I felt a little better. So I went back home. I sat down at the kitchen table, made a plan for completing my studies, developed a project for my master's thesis, sent my draft to the ethics professor, and decided to complete my studies as soon as possible. My anger dissolved my internal numbness, a new fire was burning inside me without my awareness.

All the anger, indignation, and disappointment over my friend's suicide suddenly broke over me like a tidal wave. In the case of a suicide, unlike an accidental death, the person who committed suicide can be blamed. As the most extreme degree of self-harm, suicide also causes harm to others. Thus a suicide can cause great anger and disappointment among those left behind. The problem is that the object of all this anger is absent. Anger and disappointment is spewed into a void or is projected onto one's environment, since the person who is in fact responsible is no longer present. It is important to admit to one's own anger and find a "healthy" outlet for it. Excessive anger can prevent the development of acceptance.[1] By contrast, channeled anger can have a positive effect by breaking through the powerlessness of those left behind. Feelings of strength and power can return through anger and new energy begins to soften internal numbness. The will to live also emerges in anger.[2] Thus anger can certainly unleash life-giving and life-shaping strength in the mourning process. The challenge for grief counselors is to help the grieving person not to repress their anger and together to seek ways in which it can be used as a source of energy.

1. Wagner, *Komplizierte Trauer*, 2.
2. Stülpnagel, *Warum nur?*, 90–91.

Barriers of Guilt

Feelings of guilt are among the most typical emotions that mourners wrestle with following a suicide. Most survivors wonder what they did wrong, and they often ascribe part of the responsibility for the suicide to themselves. Unfortunately, feelings of guilt prevent further steps on the path of mourning.

20. WHOSE FAULT IS SUICIDE?

Anger erupted suddenly in my mourning process, like a volcano. It was different with feelings of guilt. They were present from the first moment I learned of Angelika's suicide. At times they were latent and barely noticeable, but sometimes they dominated everything else.

For months, in countless repetitions, I reevaluated my last phone call, my last texts and emails with Angelika. Why didn't I notice anything? Should I have addressed the issue more directly? But she seemed to be doing better?! Why didn't I insist that she come to visit us during our long honeymoon and travel with us for a couple of weeks? Should I have called her psychiatrist and talked to her about the sleeping pill prescriptions? Why did I fight with Angelika six months ago? Would it have been different if not for that? But we had long since reconciled. Maybe our friendship was not good for her. I tried to find a way to deal with the question of guilt in my diary:

> In the face of Angelika's death I am continually reminded of my powerlessness. Although I have invested so much in my relationship with Angelika and have so often implored God for her life, none of that helped. Prayer, hard work, love, encouragement, and friendship—none of this could change anything in Angelika's life and prevent her death. . . . Do you know, Angelika, that I can't handle your loss so easily? I wonder what could have kept you alive? Why did your family ignore your illness? Why didn't you call when you weren't doing well? Did I fail? What should I have done to keep you here? I should have felt it and known it! Why didn't I notice anything? Her death is so pointless, such a waste of life!

For a long time I lived with the belief that I should have noticed something. I should have felt that she wanted to take her life.

When I could no longer endure blaming myself, I held internal monologues blaming Angelika's family and her broader environment. Why didn't the family do anything about the bullying Angelika faced as a child? —Then she would certainly still be alive now! How could a trained specialist, a psychiatrist, prescribe medication so thoughtlessly? —That was certainly negligent! And where were her other friends? —They should have noticed!

Chaotic, uncontrolled, and grueling, the spiral of guilt spun through my head: I had also failed . . .

Anger does not stand alone as part of the grieving process after a suicide. Feelings of guilt are also very typical.[1] I have held count-

---

1. Among others: Gill, *Suizid: Wie weiter?*, 158–59; Rauch and Rinder, *Damit aus Trauma Trauer wird*, 100–125; Stülpnagel, *Warum nur?*, 73–89; Wagner, *Komplizierte Trauer*, 47–48.

less conversations with the bereaved and in most cases, guilt and failure were central themes, even if the suicide was many years in the past. The feelings of guilt and self-blame can be overwhelming in this complicated grieving process. Conversations with oneself are often held in endless loops, outlining what one should have done differently and how one could have prevented the suicide. In order to relieve oneself somewhat, other guilty persons are often sought out. For a long time, I especially projected guilt onto Angelika's family and her therapist. The connection that I drew between their actions and the consequences was able to calm me at least a little bit, because my anger, grief, and guilt were directed toward a certain goal.

Feelings of guilt serve a function; they are connections to the deceased person. Although they are stressful, they keep the relationship alive. In addition, they protect those in mourning from the feeling of absolute powerlessness. Paradoxically, the person who committed suicide remains closer when the question of guilt is posed again and again. Memories are kept alive, since situations in which one should have noticed or done something different are replayed time and time again. At the same time, the question of guilt mitigates the feeling of abandonment and powerlessness. You are complicit, which means that you hold the reins, and thus your broken view of the world does not fall apart completely. In the long term, however, feelings of guilt prevent progress in the mourning process. Confronting the powerlessness and abandonment, the insight that the deceased person chose suicide (to the extent that reactive suicide can be called a decision) are essential elements of the grieving process.

At the beginning of the path of grief, negating questions of guilt do not help the bereaved, even less so if the people in one's surroundings actively blame the deceased. Questions of guilt may, at least at the beginning, be left unanswered, but still heard (!). Later in the mourning process it can be helpful to show those in mourning the difference between feelings of guilt and actual guilt, and to help organize these complex emotions. In addition, cognitive insight into the function of guilty feelings can also help to deal with them.[2]

2. Paul, *Schuld—Macht—Sinn*.

A Gift from God on the Path of Grief

On the path of grief, not everything can be done by one's own strength. Sometimes gifts fall into one's lap, bringing a new turning point in the process.

---

21. PICKING UP THE LIFELINE (1)—A CHANGE OF SCENERY AND SUNSHINE

In April, my partner and I decided to visit friends in Italy. A change of scenery could not hurt. So we packed up our car and drove south. Since my friend's suicide still overshadowed my life, I was not looking forward to the trip very much, nor did I hope to gain anything from it. But I love Italy, the lifestyle, the easygoing atmosphere, the food, the wine, the olive groves, and the sea. We walked through wild poppy fields, dug up edible roots, and drank good coffee. As is common in Italy, we were introduced to friends of friends and were spontaneously invited to a baptism celebration with a lavish lunch. There we met people who were actively involved in animal welfare efforts. That interested me, because I was not aware that local people advocated for the poor dogs on the streets.

Visits and celebrations continued in the following days. Among other things, we were also taken to a barbecue in the countryside. The sun was shining warmly and my inner life, numbed by death, was able to sense a little bit of life. When we arrived at the barbecue I noticed that there was nothing around except for a shell of a building, olive trees, the people celebrating. I kept slightly away from the group, observed what was happening and the surroundings, and suddenly I noticed two little puppies. They both looked anxious but still curious; they were emaciated and seemed to be very hungry. I immediately got some food from the buffet and fed the hungry dogs. Although they were afraid, they gratefully took the food and allowed me to touch them. But as soon as anyone else approached, they ran away. I asked everyone at the party if they wanted to give these abandoned puppies a home, but they only laughed at me. I spent most of the day with these two little dogs, who looked at me with big, sad eyes.

Of course I remembered that Angelika's fondest wish had always been to have a dog. It saddened me that her life had ended before this was possible. Sunk in these thoughts, at the edge of the party, these two skinny, anxious puppies seemed to me to be a wave from Angelika, a gift from God, a thin lifeline offering itself to me.

Three-quarters of a year after Angelika's suicide, during which time I had mostly withdrawn into my shell, life came to me in Italy. Although the energy and desire for a change of scenery is often lacking in the situation of grief, it can do a lot of good. In complicated mourning situations, as in the case of a suicide, it is a matter of gradually coming back into contact with something living. Slowly feeling, experiencing, and tasting that there is something more than just death, loss, and finality. In the mind of a person in grief, this hardly seems possible. That is why it is so important to be brought along into life by other people. Sometimes the mourning person is able to respond to life's helping hand, to sense the lifeline and pick it up: active resilience in response to the gifts of God and of life.

Back to Life

A person in mourning returns to life step by step, gradually and often without even noticing at first. Often you only realize in retrospect that you are in a different place than before, that something has changed.

---

22. PICKING UP THE LIFELINE (2)—A LIFELINE ON EIGHT LEGS

A thin, irrational, emotional lifeline offered itself to me here, in the middle of nowhere at a barbecue in southern Italy. While the others partied, my mind and my intuition, my rationality and my hope for change engaged in an internal battle.

But I was not always noted for my rationality. And so I quickly made my decision: I would not let these two puppies die on the street. This lifeline was here for me and the two dogs to grab! It was not easy to persuade my friends to let these dirty, emaciated street dogs into their car. And it was much more difficult to convince my partner of the plan. But both he and my friends ultimately had to resign themselves in the face of my stubbornness.

Now it was a great advantage that a few days earlier I had met animal rights activists, who helped me with cleaning and medical care for the dogs, as well as with

---

all the necessary veterinary formalities. When we finally drove back to Switzerland, we were no longer a pair, but a foursome: Simson and Levi moved in with us. Despite opposition and obstacles, I felt that this was the right decision. I was probably aware intuitively of the hidden lifeline presenting itself to me, which would draw me out of the isolation of grief bit by bit.

Back in Switzerland everything was just as it had been, and yet nothing was the same. In my normal environment, I was in danger of sinking back into grief and despair. But two things had changed: for one thing, I had experienced life beyond death and grief in Italy; and more importantly, two six-month-old, hyperactive puppies had moved in with me. It was no longer possible to hide away within my own four walls. No matter how I felt, no matter what the weather was like, these two young dogs were impossible to tire out, and so I was outside with them for three to five hours a day, meeting new people along the way.

I often thought of Angelika as I watched my two dogs playing and running. What would she have said? What would our shared walks have been like? I was certain that she would have enjoyed the two of them very much.

With Simson and Levi I began to walk my way through grief day by day: sometimes I was engrossed in internal conversations with my dead friend, sometimes I expressed accusations against God, and sometimes I simply breathed in the fresh smell of rain and smiled.

This phase of my mourning process is very particular and certainly cannot be transferred to everyone. In my case, the dogs changed the structure of my days. Circling around Angelika and her death were no longer the focal point; instead it was the two young dogs. In a quite practical sense, life returned on eight legs. In the space where Angelika had left a big hole, two dogs jumped in. They could not replace Angelika, they were nothing like her. But they were able to fill the emptiness with life. I also met new people through my dogs and so new friendships were established on my walks. Another crucial factor was added to these: movement in nature and in the fresh air.

Sometimes, unplanned events and intuitive decisions turn life upside down, and precisely in doing so allow the vicious circle of grief to burst apart. Here and there in the midst of the depths of grief lifelines appear that can be grasped and bring crucial changes. Ultimately, these things may sound banal, but a change to habitual structures, new people or animals, and movement can open new perspectives on life even in complex grieving processes.

Help along the Path of Grief

Finding one's way back to life also means being confronted with the challenges of daily life. In order to master these, those in mourning need support systems and resources of help.

> ## 23. TOOLS IN DEALING WITH THE EMOTIONAL BURDEN OF DAILY LIFE
>
> Through the energy of anger and the liveliness of the two young street dogs, I gradually felt capable of resuming and concluding my studies. I came to the following insight, which I recorded in thick letters in my diary:
>
> > My life has to go on somehow and yours simply stopped—you ended it yourself. It scares me to do something now that was not planned, that looks different than we had hoped . . .
>
> Through two of my fellow students I was brought up to date with my studies. We studied in twos and threes at home, sometimes several times a week, regardless of our individual condition in preparation for the master's exam. I rarely went to the Faculty of Theology; there were still spaces that I avoided because spending time there was too emotionally intense and laden with memories. I had fortunately completed all the required seminars before Angelika's death. In this way I was able to write the last

remaining paper as well as my master's thesis and pass all the required master's exams, and thus to complete my studies within nine months. These months consisted primarily of walking the dogs, studying, and working. These activities and the busy days helped me to briefly forget about Angelika now and then.

Exactly one year after Angelika's suicide, my life now seemed to be back to normal, viewed from the outside. But what looked "normal" from the outside was only achieved with a great internal effort. I struggled daily not to let the despair overwhelm me and just sit there completely frozen up. Memories of Angelika were constantly being called to mind. Our friendship and my studies in theology were so intertwined that the content of what I was studying often brought memories with it. . . . And we had still had many shared plans to study, plans to drink coffee together, plans for the future. Now I was alone with these plans and drank the twelve cups of coffee per day on my own. On the anniversary of Angelika's death itself, I had to get out, I could not have endured being at home. I took my dogs and went hiking, farther and farther, so that when I got home I simply fell asleep from pure exhaustion.

My longtime personal coach was a great help to me. With him I was able to create an internal system of drawers that proved to be very useful. I set aside times for despair and grief, then they were placed in a drawer and I tried to focus on the tasks of the day and studying. It took some practice before it worked. The drawer system did not always help, but I was increasingly able to avoid sinking into endless cycles of grief and emotions.

Getting back to one's own life after a suicide is a long and painful process. It often requires a conscious decision every single day to actively seek it out. There are various support systems and tools that help to cope with everyday life. Little emotional organization systems like the drawer system mentioned above. The little study group with my two fellow students has only been mentioned briefly, but it was central in my grieving process. It was a stable support system in which it was not necessary to wear a mask, the topics were defined by our common goal, and we were all working on the same thing. Hardly anything gave me so much normalcy and stability as this study group. Such "normal" places and people are unbelievably valuable in the grieving process. One's own emotional state is not in the foreground, but instead the common goal. Stable, "normal" places are worth their weight in gold for those in mourning. Places where other people are not afraid of the bereaved emotionality, but where other topics and activities are the focus, where life is lived and, for example, a common goal is worked toward or trained for.

Those who accompany mourners on this section of the journey must know how emotionally intense this phase is. The person left behind is returning to life in public, and they will enter spaces, engage in activities, and visit places that can call up memories unintentionally. For the first time, life is lived again and the absence of the deceased becomes evident in daily life.

Deconstruction
and Reconstruction

Through profound life events like the loss of a beloved person through suicide, one's own personal (religious) system of meaning is called into question. Beliefs and convictions may prove to be no longer viable, so that they must be fundamentally reexamined and adapted.

24. WHAT CAN I STILL BELIEVE?

Angelika's suicide gradually called into question not only my life, my studies, my every day, and my future, but also my personal beliefs. I found the following passage from this period in my diary:

> I don't know any more what I believe in: who is God? What is church? What endures? Much in my life does not seem to exist anymore. Things that appeared so unshakable have dissolved into nothing.

For many years I had worked in a reformed church as a volunteer and later was employed as a youth worker; I was on my way to becoming a pastor, was at the end of my studies in theology, but all my beliefs, my system of meaning, seemed to have collapsed. As with an onion, layer after layer began to peel off; sometimes I was conscious of this, but often I was not. This process lasted for months and many of my questions and searching even occupied me for years.

My previous image of the church had already dissolved through my disappointment. I lost (fortunately) the belief that perfect community and unbroken places exist in this world. But it went further: traditional worship services had always been too constricting and dusty for me, and not much changed on that point. But with the more modern forms of worship, it was above all the songs and the cheerfulness that I could no longer bear and that became foreign to me. Everything seemed too superficial and remote from the realities of life. For example, one song goes, "I will worship you in my darkest hour, I will worship you when I am out of power . . ." How was that supposed to work? I was not Paul, who still sang songs and preached while in prison. I knew that I did not sing songs of praise to God in my dark hours; at best, there were laments, accusations, and often silence.

My image of God was also deconstructed, or perhaps better: expanded. It became more multifaceted and diffuse. I did not turn away from the Christian faith, but from the many images of God and practices I had inherited. God had to be more than "my friend" and certainly not just male. How do you hold worship services if you can't stand them? What do you pray when you are without words? These and many other questions gradually emerged and rotated through my mind. I did not want to become godless. But I had to find new or different forms of faith for myself in this phase of grief. Thus I discovered, for example, the Benedictine Liturgy of the Hours. What deeply touched me was the Vespers sung in Latin in Einsiedeln Abbey.

My prayers seemed irrelevant, and most often I had no words to pray. So rather than force myself into empty prayers, I battled word by word with my speechlessness until this prayer offered itself as a text in my diary:

> I look to heaven tired and empty; I am body, shell, dust, bones;
> But is what I cannot do done in me? Does what seems dead, move?
> Only through God, through her power
> She nurses the place, creates hope
> I raise my eyes
> to the light, the light is inside me.

I learned that faith is often searching, asking, not knowing, and struggling. Hoping for something that one does not know and yet somehow senses. Searching for something that creates hope inside oneself and moves one very personally. Something that cannot be grasped and nevertheless is outlined in the Bible and in the history of the church, in images and texts. After a failed attempt to find words for a prayer, I wrote in my diary,

> There is also a lot of hope in me. I believe that I will see Angelika again, but first I have to live, I get to live, and I may hope and I may trust that my life will have a positive influence in this world.

What is presented here as a short text is in reality a multifaceted, years-long journey: doubt—learning to believe again—questioning—daring to trust. . . . This path continues even now, for my personal belief system was called into question by the experience of grief and was reframed over many years: from a supposed possession of the right faith to a questioning hope.

For religious people, the deconstruction of beliefs can be a painful process in working through a suicide. After a suicide, there is often not much certainty left—but the core that remains also crystalizes in the process. Everything that is superficial and insincere is washed away. In this process, the question of theodicy must also be allowed to be asked. Accusations against God are already common in biblical texts, and it is all the more acceptable to express them today. Texts such as Jeremiah 12:1–6, Psalms 49 and 73, for example, protest against God because evil people do well in life and the righteous do poorly. The most forceful accusations, doubts, and criticisms against God are found in the book of Job. Although there is no answer to the question of why people suffer, nevertheless, Job only recognizes God after he is able to doubt and complain: "I had heard of you by the hearing of the ear, but now my eye sees you" (Job 42:5). Deconstructing religion offers the opportunity to learn new and different forms of faith and to find one's own language for it. Openness and readiness for dialogue, especially in relation to religious upheavals, are helpful for people in grief. That is, it can be helpful when people are permitted to doubt, search, ask questions, and discuss together and not be steamrolled by religious expectations. Rigid religious beliefs hinder the course of processing, for example, when pastors or spiritual advisors prescribe what is theologically right and wrong, which images of God are legitimate, and leave no room for anger and doubt.

Pastors and spiritual advisors who know that faith can never offer absolute assurances, but is simply a questioning existence between refutation and certainty,[1] are able to be very helpful in this phase. The next steps in the process are supported when one is permitted to talk about doubts or processes of searching without fear of judgment, as personal faith and a religious system of meaning can be a great resource in the grieving process.

1. H. Luther, *Religion und Alltag*, 23.

Accepting and Integrating

Many small steps are required before it is again possible to develop desires for one's own future. It takes time and support for those in mourning to build new paths from the debris that remains.

25. HOLDING THE PAINTBRUSH IN YOUR HANDS

Life went on, I completed my studies, and two years after Angelika's suicide I began my vicarage year, the period of practical training as a pastor. This year of training was the last year that we had planned together in detail. We had many wishes, dreams, and ideas about the future for the time after that. Things that we had hoped to be able to do, such as eventually sharing a pastorate. But this vicarage year, it would have been something we shared! I now became aware of this in many situations: during the weeks of coursework there were two-person rooms, and we had agreed to room together throughout the year. In addition, I had accepted a long commute in order to be near to where Angelika wanted to do her training. We had planned to spend lunch breaks together and to prepare our sermons in her apartment. I had to let go of much that we would have shared and organize things differently than we had planned.

It felt as though I was standing in front of a screen. The image that was supposed to appear was already sketched out in fine detail. But now I had to take a paint-brush, ignore the sketch, and paint my own, new picture with different colors and shapes. Fortunately, there were people who showed me new "painting techniques" and opened the way to other plans for my life. The new pic-ture was painted with tears at the beginning, sometimes with despair and reluctance, and again and again with anger. I had to let go of something I had no desire to let go of. I found this period difficult, the coursework was sometimes nearly unbearable, and my thoughts repeat-edly wandered to Angelika, who should have been there too. At the same time I learned to accept that things were now different than I had planned.

After the vicarage year, life really took off again. I found a position as a pastor, moved multiple times with my partner, met new people, began to pursue my doctorate, wandered through forests and fields with my dogs, planned and organized study trips, began to gar-den, spent time in the monastery, etc.

There were moments when Angelika's absence was still unbearable. But over the years a new, different picture of life emerged—my own picture. Once, when I was again uncertain where to paint the lines, I wrote in my diary,

> I am standing here and don't actually know anymore what a person is. I have the feeling that some of what I thought I knew is gone, is no longer so. I feel empty inside, in a positive way. I'm on an internal search through new, unknown terrain. Everywhere I am discovering new ideas, feeling how they grow or dissolve in the air. I find myself on a walk through

life, discovering new plants and animals, a completely new environment. The light shines differently on my path, muted and lighter on the pathless terrain. I smell the fresh, invigorating air, but do not know where I am going. No, it does not scare me to be so pathless. I feel how curiosity invigorates me, gives me joy in life. The waiting and searching does not bother me. I no longer need to take the old path that I have tread so often, the one I know by heart. I can breathe freely, discover things anew, let go of the old, and be searching.

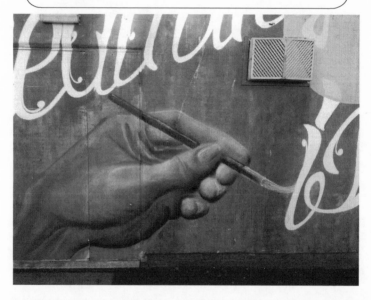

Similarly to a sudden death, many things are left open after a suicide. Those left behind stand there and look at the shared plans and dreams, which now are in shambles. "The unpredictable and un-plannable finitude of life that every death marks always renders life a fragment."[1] It is a challenge to once again become active and to allow something new and different to develop from the fragments. Often what stands in the way is the fear that the person who committed suicide could be forgotten. However, this section

1. H. Luther, *Religion und Alltag*, 168.

of the journey is not about forgetting the deceased or repressing memories, but accepting the death and nevertheless living again. One's own life can and must somehow continue, even if those in mourning have to struggle with what that should look like. The future is like a construction site, the past is a ruin.[2] Rebuilding one's life is now a matter of integrating the memories and emotions into the new construct of life. As was the case with me, a certain curiosity can suddenly set in at this stage and letting go of the old can be freeing. During this time, support persons can be a sounding board for the bereaved by supporting them as they clear their own path of all the rubble and, together with the person in mourning, exploring their dreams for the future, their ideas, and desires.

2. H. Luther, *Religion und Alltag*, 168–69.

Sacred Objects and Sacred Moments

Even after many years, survivors of suicide experience moments when they are assailed by melancholy, they pause for a moment and remember the deceased. Even when daily life becomes normalized, everything has still changed.

26. EVERYTHING STAYS DIFFERENT

Even as the years passed, Angelika remained present in my memories. There were moments in which I missed her immensely or she was suddenly very near. In my normal, everyday life there were and are so many things that remind me of her. A few of these things are described in the three unconnected sections that follow.

I was at the confirmation camp, the kids had some free time and I wanted to grab a coffee. Three of my young leaders came up to me and wanted to convince me to play foosball with them. This idea struck me like lightning. I had not played since Angelika's death, for nearly five years. It seemed like a betrayal to play foosball without her. And she had given us a voucher for a foosball table for our wedding—which she could no longer redeem. Hesitantly, I nevertheless agreed, the youths' persuasive efforts were persistent. It was fun to play again. As soon as I got home, I enthusiastically told my partner about the foosball table and my idea of buying one for ourselves. The next day we went out and found a store nearby that sold such equipment. Only twenty-four hours after my return from the confirmation camp there was a foosball table in our home. Even today it occupies a prominent place in our living room and brings joy not only to us but also to our guests.

Two years after Angelika's death I discovered a plant in a friend's apartment. I froze inside and saw Angelika in my mind's eye. The memories were very vivid, very close. I immediately recognized the plant that I had been searching for for years, but did not know what it was called. Angelika used to have that kind of plant in her apartment. We were both fascinated by it but did not know the botanical name. So Angelika called it "Cuc" for short, since its stem looked like a cucumber. Angelika had promised me a cutting from Cuc, since I liked it so much. But that never happened. So now I found this plant completely unexpectedly in my friend's living room, and she was also able to tell me the name. When I got home, I searched the internet until I finally came across the plants and seeds in Germany and had some delivered. There are still several Cucs (Madagascar Jewels) in my apartment, which keep the memory of Angelika alive and make me smile.

In a kitchen cupboard, way at the back and somewhat hidden, there are two identical orange-yellow-red mugs. My partner once served tea in these mugs. I angrily told him that they are not allowed to be used, since during our time as roommates Angelika and I always had our coffee and spooned the foamed milk out of them. We bring the mugs with us in every move, but they are not used even today. But when I see them I remember with a smile how Angelika had ordered us both a cup of foamed milk at a restaurant. And so the foamed milk that I always have on my coffee is also a reminder of her.

Even today, over a decade later, I sometimes pause and wonder what she might say? What would she be doing? What would her life be like? It remains open. . . . And everything stays different.

For relatives and friends it is not easy to understand the unexpected reactions of those in mourning in certain situations. My partner had no idea why I snapped when he took a mug out of the cupboard seven years after Angelika's suicide. Reactions of grief are neither rational nor bound to temporal limits. In the middle of life, one is unexpectedly and suddenly confronted with memories of the deceased and overwhelmed by them. The challenge for those left behind after a suicide is not to freeze in the face of memories, but instead to integrate them into one's life. It is worthwhile pursuing impulses that can be helpful for processing, even if they seem strange from the outside. For the bereaved, objects can be sacred and can lead to healing moments by keeping memories alive in a positive way and allowing something new to develop from them. Such as the Madagascar Jewels that grow and thrive in our home. Or the foosball table, where my partner pulled out all the stops to find one for us. Sometimes even objects or actions of people close to you can lead to sacred moments. Moments in which the soul of the mourner heals a bit.

Rituals and Reconciliation

Grief and reconciling oneself with the situation take their own time. Rituals help to mark these transitions and to appreciate them physically and psychologically.

27. TIME TRAVEL AND RECONCILIATION

Almost ten years after Angelika's suicide, I spent four months working in California. When my partner visited me, we rented a car for a few days. It was soon clear what the destination of our trip should be. So we drove off heading northeast. We stayed overnight in Las Vegas and the next evening arrived at Bryce Canyon. It was already dark and on the way we had driven through a snowstorm, so we went straight to our hotel room. I did not really know why I wanted to go back there. But in these last ten years, the same scenes had come to mind again and again, like in a film:

Bryce Canyon with its enchanting, bizarre beauty . . . the fantastic lookout point that had astonished me . . . the missed call from Angelika's number on my phone . . . my unease and returning the call immediately . . . no one answers . . . back in the cheap, dark motel, another attempt to call Angelika . . . finally someone picks up. —Angelika's father tells me that she is dead.

My internal numbness over Angelika's suicide, my complicated path of grief, it all began at Bryce Canyon. The images of this park had been linked with my emotions and burned themselves into my memories.

The next morning, wrapped in the warmest clothes we had brought from southern California, my partner and I made our way into the park. We started exploring Bryce Canyon from the very end and in the frigid cold we hiked through the bizarre moonscape dusted with snow. We gradually worked our way back to the park entrance until we came to the exact lookout point I had feared.

It was late afternoon, similar to ten years previously, but it was winter and the clouds were lying over Bryce Canyon. The view was breathtaking: white snow on the red rock formations. I had never seen this place like this . . .

Having come to this point after ten years, I needed some time to myself. I stood there, tears running down my cheeks. Once again I went over the internal film of the last ten years of my mourning process: the shock and numbness, later the despair and weariness with life, I felt the grief and anger, but most of all I was aware of Angelika's absence. There was so much that would have brought her joy, that would have made it worth living. I stood there, reflecting, and held a last internal dialogue with my deceased friend. I felt that it was now time to let her go entirely. In this moment, the clouds broke apart and sunbeams struck the rocks, my face, and my thoughts. A bird flew by in the direction of the sun. I opened my hands and spread out my arms, as though I had let this bird fly away. I prayed, said goodbye to my dear friend, and entrusted her to God. Sad, liberated, and somewhat confused I went back to my partner and hugged him. Together we stayed for a bit at the lookout point and admired the beauty of nature.

Not everyone needs to return to the place where the "deadly reality" struck them, where the path of grief unwillingly began. But for me it was important to be able to stand at the lookout point again and to create a new internal film. One with clouds breaking apart and a bird flying free over a sugar-dusted canyon. This reframing was necessary to completely break through the internal numbness of that time and to create new images and memories, in order to think back on Angelika. But even more importantly, it was necessary to return in order to truly say "à dieu" after all those years and entrust Angelika to God.

Paths of mourning are individual and long routes. I had not planned a farewell or a ritual, but it emerged spontaneously from the situation. Rituals and farewells that integrate body, soul, and spirit can have a lasting impact. They can change emotions and thinking, can work as catalysts. Rituals are "structural aids of faith. They help individuals to cope with the transitions of life that are sometimes hopeful, sometimes difficult, and sometimes associated with crisis."[1] They do this by creating sacred moments in which an

---

1. Ziemer, *Seelsorgelehre*, 252.

effect is developed, (internal) conflicts are resolved, and identity is bolstered. In addition, new and different memories and narratives emerge in rituals.[2] Which rituals prove to be more helpful at which times depends primarily on the bereaved person. Religions and literature on mourning contain a stock of countless helpful rituals. But sometimes it is necessary to invent a ritual for oneself that fits the specific situation and transcends it. Sometimes those in mourning are only able to really let go and reconcile with life years later. Marking this moment ritually means setting an anchor that will hold fast even in the storms of daily life.

2. Hoffmann, *Understanding Religious Ritual*, 3.

Finding the Words Again

Regaining the ability to articulate oneself in the face of a suicide means taking a step on the path toward healing and allowing other people to participate in it.

28. CONTINUING THE NARRATIVE

It took more than a decade to put this path of mourning into words as it stands here. I have told many stories, opened windows onto my heart and my thoughts, described processes of grief. Angelika's suicide is long since past. Memories have faded, and a large part of grief is behind me. My life plan has taken on new and different contours than I thought it would at that time.

Life goes on, with joys, sorrows, work, challenges, with friendships and a lot of coffee. My thoughts no longer wander to Angelika several times a day. Sometimes I even forget who she was to me for a couple of days. But never for long, and then I sit there, as I do tonight, drink my coffee and think wistfully of Angelika. Of her gentle nature, her empathy, the serious conversations and funny moments and of all the days that were not lived. I miss her. She left a hole behind. Everything is still different.

> And yet her loss is no longer an open, festering and oozing wound. Her suicide and the complicated process of grief have left their mark. I am more hesitant to make friends. I know that life runs out like sand through your fingers. Loss, grief, and pain have marked and shaped me. That does not stop me from seeking life, playing with my dogs, and giving myself trustingly into the hands of the Holy Spirit. An empty space will remain, and perhaps that's a good thing.

And now?

Really dead. Yes, really and truly dead. A suicide is deadly real, hard, clear, and strikes like the blow of a hammer. Finding my own words for this hard reality and opening helpful doors for others' mourning process was originally the aim of the blog. I hoped that my experiences and thoughts might create verbal bridges for others. Perhaps the stone walls of silence would crack here and there? I wish this for you and for me. Telling our personal stories, which others have experienced in the same way and yet very differently, creates connectedness and understanding. So I would like to become more articulate myself and with my words contribute to others' ability to express themselves. Now I have come to the end, I would like to encourage you to continue with your narrative, telling your story as you encounter the suicide, the grief, and the loss. To tell your own stories, to paint, or to write. To call the "deadly reality" by its name, in order not to suffocate in the silence. I want to encourage you that your story can continue by telling it, on your path of grief or in your work with those in mourning. Continue the narrative, so that the deadly reality does not lead to loneliness and silence, but to sympathy, understanding, and perhaps even to reconciliation with what has been experienced.

Suicide in Theology and Pastoral Care

The stigmatization that many survivors fear and often experience even today is grounded in a tradition over a thousand years old. For a long time suicide was a great sin. The deceased were not buried in a graveyard and officially they were not allowed to be mourned. Relatives and the bereaved were thus also exposed to ostracism and stigmatization. This was the case even though suicides have always been a part of human history. Even the Bible expresses suicidal thoughts and recounts suicides. In addition, care for those left behind by suicide is a part of spiritual care and pastoral praxis.

THEOLOGICAL PERSPECTIVES

There are texts in the Bible that express suicidal thoughts and intentions (e.g., Jonah 4:8; Jer 15:10; Job 3:3) or depict suicide itself (e.g., Samson in Judg 16:30; Saul in 1 Sam 31:4; Judas in Matt 27:5). It is striking that these are sometimes narrated in detail, but are not given value judgments. In early Christianity, too, suicide was not regarded as reprehensible and there was not always a clear line between martyrdom and suicide. In the Christian tradition suicide was first explicitly condemned by Augustine. He considered suicide to be a violation of the fifth commandment: "You shall not murder" (Deut 5:17). "In the context of a time that regarded religious suicide as a special form of martyrdom and of the Stoa, which supported 'the ideal of self-controlled dying,' Augustine found himself forced to intervene against suicidal acts."[1] Augustine's opinion prevailed and beginning with the Council of Arles (ca. 553 CE) suicide was regarded as a crime and caused by the devil. Beginning with the First Council of Braga in 561, suicides were denied burial by the church. At the Sixteenth Council of Toledo in 693, a temporary excommunication of two months was imposed as punishment for an attempted suicide, and ultimately in 860 Pope Nicholas I declared suicide to be a deadly sin.[2] This led to suicide being regarded as a reprehensible act for the next thousand years and beyond. The debate over what a suicide is, from a theological perspective, continues until today. For example, in the last century theologians such as Karl Barth and Dietrich Bonhoeffer commented on suicide and rejected it on the basis of nuanced argumentation.[3]

The doctrinal teaching of the church had impacts on legislation in various countries. Condemnation of suicide itself and attempted suicide were only removed from criminal codes through the Enlightenment. In the UK, for example, failed suicide attempts were not decriminalized until 1961.[4] The Roman Catholic Church did not allow suicides to be buried in hallowed ground until 1983 in the Codex Iuris Canonici.[5]

The desire to evaluate suicide with dogmatic categories is, in my opinion, neither appropriate to the subject nor helpful for those left behind by suicide or those who have survived an attempted suicide.[6] The biblical attitude is rather more helpful: as mentioned above, from a biblical perspective neither suicide itself nor suicidal thoughts are condemned; they are rather recognized and taken seriously as a reality of life. The focus is on the person

1. Hoheisel and Christ-Friedrich, "Suizid," 442–53.
2. Hoheisel and Christ-Friedrich, "Suizid," 442–53.
3. Hoheisel and Christ-Friedrich, "Suizid," 448.
4. "Suicide Act 1961."
5. Lind, *Selbstmord in der Frühen Neuzeit*, 21–39.
6. On this cf. also Ziemer, *Seelsorgelehre*, 323.

who is suffering, whom nothing and no one can separate from the love of God (Rom 8:38–39). The same applies to those left behind by suicide. This certainty can bring consolation in the deepest grief and loneliness. For "grief leads us to places that we ourselves have not sought out. . . . Grief leads us into the desert, to the edge of life. And it takes a long time before we recognize that in the desert we encounter two things simultaneously—loneliness and the closeness of God."[7] A classic pastoral story of mourning is the road to Emmaus (Luke 24:13–39). There, Jesus Christ appears as a pastor himself, who accompanies, has compassion, listens, asks questions, remains present, and ultimately opens a new path in which despair and sadness give way to the hope of resurrection and the freedom of creation. The biblical tradition can offer a rich source of comfort and support for those on the path of mourning, for in the biblical proclamation "images and motifs are presented . . . that express more than any correct statement, no matter how carefully considered."[8] Biblical texts have the ability to change perceptions and value judgments, and can thus offer a healing impetus on the path of mourning.

PASTORAL CARE AS SUPPORT FOR SURVIVORS

Dealing with dying, death, suicide, and grief is a recurring theme in pastoral practice. This spans the spectrum from emergency counseling to years-long bereavement support, especially when a death is entirely unexpected and/or is caused by the deceased or someone else. Anyone who works as a pastor or supports people in other roles will inevitably be confronted with the topic of suicide. Especially in the case of a suicide, support for those left behind does not end with the funeral. In the sense of follow-up care, which is at the same time suicide prevention, it is essential to closely support those left behind following a suicide. Where this is not possible, contact should nevertheless be maintained.

7. Schibilsky, *Trauerwege*, 107.
8. Schibilsky, *Trauerwege*, 243.

In addition, it is advisable to point the bereaved toward self-help groups, specialists, and therapeutic options, and to encourage them to take advantage of these opportunities. It can be helpful to offer to accompany them to a first meeting.

Pastoral activity has recently given more attention to the suffering of the person who committed suicide. Thus the question of whether suicide is to be classified as a sin is no longer central; rather, the focus is on solidarity with the desperate person and with those in mourning who have been left behind. "Judgment is increasingly giving way to sympathy."[9] However, supporting the bereaved in this situation is not easy, as those in mourning can react dismissively, hurt, or with a sudden withdrawal. Grief support requires persistence, theoretical knowledge, and sensitivity. Spiritual advisors face the challenge of recognizing and possibly supporting the various, individual reactions of grief and coping strategies.[10] An understanding of pastoral care that is rooted in the Christian faith and places importance on the aspects of support, encounters, and the interpretation of one's life can do justice to this task.[11]

Pastoral care for survivors of suicide is supportive care. In this the person in mourning experiences that someone else feels and walks with them in the powerlessness, the incomprehensibility, and loneliness, as on the road to Emmaus in the Gospel of Luke (Luke 24). This companionship provides comfort and the gospel is able to take shape in a difficult situation. The goal is a discursive reification of the biblical image of God in the context of the individual situation of mourning.[12] At the same time, pastoral care is not only support, but also encounter: two people come into contact on eye level. In addition, the aspect of the foreign is always present. The otherness of individuals can provide a new and different impetus that can lead to a shift of perspective and guide

---

9. Gill, *Suizid: Wie weiter?*, 35.

10. Among others Lammer, *Trauer verstehen*, 22.

11. Klessmann, *Seelsorge*.

12. Ziemer, *Seelsorgelehre*, 110–11.

people on the path to freedom (Gal 5:1).[13] This is linked with the third point, interpreting life in the horizon of the Christian system of meaning. In their office or their commission, pastors represent the Christian faith.[14] The fundamental Christian attitude becomes relevant when those left behind by suicide are supported in coping with daily life and a frame of reference is offered that helps to accomplish the work of orienting oneself in one's own biography (of grief).[15]

Rituals can provide a helpful impetus for processing in this work. Since commonly known rituals have increasingly lost significance and awareness in the course of society's individualization, pastors and the bereaved are often faced with the challenge of creating helpful rituals that are relevant to the situation. Concrete actions and rituals help both to accept the loss and to create a new life plan in the long term. When the bereaved show signs of being strongly affected and symptoms of complicated mourning, it is recommended to seek help from a therapist or support in a self-help group.[16] Even virtual communities of mourners, such as can be found on Facebook, can be a daily source of support.

13. Meyer-Blanck and Weyel, *Studien- und Arbeitsbuch Praktische Theologie*, 155; Ziemer, *Seelsorgelehre*, 114–15.

14. Fechtner et al., *Praktische Theologie*, 189.

15. Meyer-Blanck and Weyel, *Studien- und Arbeitsbuch Praktische Theologie*, 146; Ziemer, *Seelsorgelehre*, 117–18.

16. Hausmann, *Einführung in die Psychotraumatologie*, 127–28.

Theory of Grief

Grief itself is psychological and physical work that involves cognitive, emotional, motoric, and physiological aspects.[1] It is dealing with loss and one's own fears and experiences that rattle and hurt a person.[2] Grief is coping with loss and can be regarded as a dynamic process of adapting to a reality that has been radically altered by a death. It is a matter of adjusting to the loss and, where possible, finding new purpose in life.[3]

Very generally, grief is about accepting the pain, recognizing the altered reality, and ultimately creating one's life path anew. It is characteristic of the mourning process that the pain over the loss and the intense emotions gradually decline. Nevertheless, mourning processes often last much longer than previously thought—so three to five years is completely normal.

GRIEF AFTER A SUICIDE

More often than with other kinds of death in which someone has died of natural causes, grief in the case of a suicide can be overwhelming. It can lie like a veil over one's entire life and for a long time can swallow up every joy, social contact, and the will to live. Discussions of grief are increasingly asking what constitutes

1. Wagner, *Komplizierte Trauer*, 4.
2. Gerlitz et al., "Trauer," 4–27.
3. Ziemer, *Seelsorgelehre*, 305.

"normal" and "complicated"[4] grief. A consensus criterion was first proposed in 1997, "which differs qualitatively from depression and anxiety and predicts a clinically relevant impairment. The main symptoms of the consensus criterion were defined by 1) the stress of separation and 2) traumatic stress."[5] Various factors, such as the circumstances of death and lack of social support, can make the process of mourning more difficult, resulting in a complicated grief process. This differs from normal grief especially in its length and in the following seven predicative symptoms: 1. intrusions, 2. emotional pain, 3. longing for the deceased person, 4. feelings of loneliness and the feeling of emptiness, 5. avoidance behavior, 6. sleep disorders, 7. social withdrawal.[6] Not all those left behind after a suicide develop symptoms of complicated grief. Nevertheless, its prevalence is striking. "In a study with predominantly female relatives of people who had committed suicide, a diagnosis of complicated grief was found in 43 percent of the participants. In particular, children with 80 percent, spouses with 78 percent, and parents with 67 percent showed the highest rates of prevalence of complicated grief."[7] Even if no symptoms of complicated grief appear, the mourning process of those left behind by suicide differs qualitatively from grief following other kinds of death. The bereaved often suffer from feelings of shame and guilt, from stigmatization, and from the fact that the circumstances of death are (or have to be) kept secret.

PHASES, TASKS, AND PATHS OF GRIEF

There are many theories for the process of mourning. These theories tend to prefer models of phases, paths, or tasks. In *phase*

4. This terminology is not used uniformly and in recent years has repeatedly been adapted. Thus various terms are currently in use in the academic context: Pathologische Trauer, Komplizierte Trauer, Traumatische Trauer, Prolongierte Trauer. Wagner, *Komplizierte Trauer*, 14–16.

5. Wagner, *Komplizierte Trauer*, 17.

6. Wagner, *Komplizierte Trauer*, 16.

7. Wagner, *Komplizierte Trauer*, 45.

models the process of grief is divided into phases with specific characteristics.[8] The strength of these models is that they provide a plausible explanation for the various emotional states of grief. They also have an orienting character. Their weakness, however, is that they oversimplify and render individual processes uniform and normative. The process of grief is not linear, nor is it experienced in the same order by everyone.[9] In addition, phase models have elements that deprive the person in mourning of autonomy, as they are apparently incapable of independent action and are at the mercy of the various phases.

Newer models increasingly understand mourning as a *task*. Their focus lies on coping with the changes and problems that a death brings.[10] They also have an orienting character, but leave more room for individual approaches and forms of grief. Models that understand grief as a task have an empowering effect because they convey a sense of practicability. Grief becomes a challenge rather than an overwhelming demand. This can have positive effects for those bereaved by a suicide, since a suicide displaces one's environment into numbness and powerlessness. However, the models of mourning tasks are also normative in that they define the tasks. Their weakness lies precisely in their understanding of practicability. Grieving is not a to-do list in which tasks can simply be completed and checked off. Task models can overwhelm those in mourning with pressure (to achieve). In addition, they suggest a practicability that is not always there.

There are many more models of grief between these two poles. One that combines the models of phases and tasks is Schibilsky's

---

8. Among others Kast, *Trauern*. Kast divides the phases as follows: denial, forceful emotions, searching and parting, a new relation to oneself and to the world. Kübler-Ross, *Interviews mit Sterbenden*. According to Kübler-Ross the phases consist of: denial, anger, negotiating, depression, acceptance. Spiegel, *Der Prozeß des Trauerns*. Spiegel identifies the individual phases of his model as follows: shock, control, regression, adaption.

9. Lammer, *Trauer verstehen*, 19.

10. Among others Lammer, *Trauer verstehen*; Worden, *Grief Counseling and Grief Therapy*.

somewhat older *spiral model*.[11] The spiral model works with more flexible transitions than the phase model and integrates the tasks of grief as part of the process of the path. This model is oriented more around the character of those in mourning. Grief is described as a path whose structure depends on the personality of the bereaved. This further breaks down normative aspects and tasks are diversified and individualized.

Ultimately, all models have their strengths and weaknesses. They are outlines that seek to explain and describe in broad strokes complicated, emotional processes. Like signposts on a trail they indicate the direction and approximate distances, but only roughly express the actual and individual nature of the path.

11. Schibilsky, *Trauerwege.*

Statistical Information

According to the WHO, there were about eight hundred thousand registered deaths by suicide worldwide in 2017. This dark number could be significantly higher. Globally, suicide is the second leading cause of death among young people aged fifteen to twenty-nine.[1] Suicide accounts for 50 percent of all violent deaths in males and 71 percent in females. Worldwide, suicide rates are highest among people over the age of seventy. People who have previously attempted suicide have a statistically higher risk of dying by suicide.[2] In Switzerland, for every completed suicide there are ten to fifteen medically treated suicide attempts. Here, too, this dark number is likely much higher. In 2014, nearly thirteen people per one hundred thousand residents died of suicide, with the rate among men three times that among women. Every year, more than a thousand people die by suicide in Switzerland. If one assumes that for each suicide at least six to ten relatives and friends are strongly affected, that means that every year at least six to ten thousand people left behind by suicide stand at the beginning of a long and complicated mourning process.[3] Many of these bereaved suffer in silence. They are silent because they have feelings of guilt or fear of stigmatization. They are silent because they have often experienced that those around them are completely overwhelmed when they speak of the deceased. Or they are silent because grief

1. World Health Organization, "Suicide."
2. World Health Organization, *Preventing Suicide.*
3. Wagner, *Komplizierte Trauer*, 43.

has no place in society and they have no idea how many people around them have experienced something similar. For many years, I also did not talk about my friend's suicide. When I began to talk about suicide as a pastor in confirmation classes, the response was significant. I noticed the same thing among my friends: once the taboo was broken, I discovered how many people in my surroundings had lost family members, friends, and relatives to suicide. Every path of grief was different and yet I recognized many similarities.

Specialist Agencies and Support Services

If you yourself are in need . . .
In case of suicidal thoughts, the first place to seek help can be family doctors, pastors, or the following contacts:

Austria

__ Counseling by phone
Telephone 142, website: www.telefonseelsorge.at

__ Austria-wide emergency number for children and youth
Telephone 147, http://rataufdraht.orf.at

Germany

__ Counseling by phone
By telephone 0800 111 0 111 or 0800 111 0 222,
www.telefonseelsorge.de

Switzerland

__ Die Dargebotene Hand ("The offered hand")
By telephone at 143 and online counseling, www.143.ch

__ Seelsorge.net
A program of the Reformed and Catholic Churches of Switzerland, seelsorge@seelsorge.net, www.seelsorge.net

United Kingdom

__ 999 and 112 is the national emergency number in the United Kingdom

__ 111, Option 2, is the National Health Services' First Response Service for mental health crises and support. This is not available in all areas of the country yet.

__ Samaritans (http://www.samaritans.org/) is a registered charity aimed at providing emotional support to anyone in distress or at risk of suicide throughout the United Kingdom.[35] They provide a 24/7, toll-free crisis line, as well as local branches.

United States

__ The National Suicide Prevention Lifeline (http://suicidepreventionlifeline.org/) is a twenty-four-hour, toll-free, confidential suicide prevention hotline available to anyone in suicidal crisis or emotional distress.

__ 911 is the national emergency number in the United States.

SELF-HELP GROUPS

Switzerland

__ Nebelmeer ("Sea of fog")
Perspectives after the suicide of a parent: self-help groups in Bern, Biel, and Zurich for twelve- to thirty-year-olds. www.nebelmeer.net

____ Verein Refugium ("Refuge Association")
Association for survivors after suicide,
Lindenbühl, 3635 Uebeschi, telephone 0848 00 18 88, info@
verein-refugium.ch,
www.verein-refugium.ch

____ Verein Trauernetz ("Grief Network Association")
Counseling, networking, and education for specialists,
founding of self-help groups, Höhestrasse 80, 8702 Zollikon,
telephone 076 598 45 30, http://trauernetz.ch

Germany

____ AGUS e. V. Angehörige um Suizid ("Relatives affected by
suicide")
Telephone 0921 150 03 80, www.agus-selbsthilfe.de

____ Federal association "Verwaiste Eltern und trauernder
Geschwister in Deutschland e. V." ("Bereaved Parents and
Siblings in Mourning in Germany, e.V."),
Roßplatz 8a, 04103 Leipzig, telephone 03419 468 884, kon-
takt@veid.de, www.veid.de

Austria

____ Emergency Psychological Service Austria (NDÖ) telephone
0699 188 55 400, www.notfallpsychologie.at

____ Austrian Society for Suicide Prevention
Self-help groups for the bereaved after suicide in Austria,
www.suizidpraevention.at

Afterword

When I read Sabrina Müller's blog about the suicide of her best friend and living with this deeply shocking experience for the first time, it touched me deeply and did not let me go for a long time. And that's why, during our next collegial conversation, I encouraged her to collect these very personal blog posts and make them into a book. Now here it is: a good, helpful, urgently needed book. What is it that impresses me—as a New Testament scholar, pastor, Christian, and contemporary—and moves me to reflect and continue?

First, I'm impressed by the honesty and sincerity. Sabrina Müller articulates what is often kept quiet in our society, including among Christians, what is hidden behind closed doors and stony or even smiling facades. She writes about the phases in which she herself lacked the words and her own faith fell into deep crises, and she writes about what was able to help her and to open her mouth again, even if there are things that will always remain incomprehensible. This very thing can also help others to endure the questionableness of our lives and our society and to support those who need it in the right way. It is only with such sincerity that Christian churches and congregations can open the space in which contemporaries, with their cares and burdens, find people to listen to and walk with them, the space in which the good news of acceptance by the life-loving God can be heard.

As an academic, I am impressed by the careful and well-considered interweaving of personal reappraisal and professional reflection. While academic literature often remains in the ivory tower of theory and explanations and the genre of self-help and parish literature often lacks critical reflection, in this book Sabrina Müller carefully intertwines these two different genres. She allows her readers to participate in her own process of mourning, provides insight into the many questions that friends and relatives affected by suicide ask themselves, and thus awakens a sensitivity for dealing with those at risk for and those left behind by suicide. And at the same time, this very personal account is placed in the horizon of psychology and pastoral doctrine, empirical research and theological reflection. Readers can also choose to follow just one strand or another, or at any point to look at individual stations in the process. This arrangement accommodates the fact that those affected by suicide can often only absorb these stories and ideas that impact them in small portions, because any more would be overwhelming. At the same time, in this book a budding academic teacher demonstrates in the best way how Practical Theology can work—as a critical-reflective support for spiritual and ecclesial praxis.

Ultimately this book is a spirited expression of the gospel, the good news from God, who—as the message of the New Testament describes it—personally cares for those who have lost themselves in life (as described in the parable of the lost sheep in Luke 15) and invites those weighed down by the burden of life to a refreshing spring (as expressed in Jesus's call of invitation in Matt 11:28–30). It is an example of faith that is able to borrow words of lament from the language of the Psalms in times of incomprehension and deepest grief and, like Job, can defiantly hurl its questions and accusations at God, particularly where the pious and sometimes clever know-it-alls (like Job's friends) have become unbearable and ultimately fail. And it is a testament to the trust that even in the depths of our life and death someone is there who is with us and takes our place, Christ, who bore the cross and all the crosses of this world so that new hope and new life would be opened to humanity, so that the light shines even in the darkness (John 1:5).

AFTERWORD

This book is a spirited and helpful book, and I hope and wish that it reaches those people who need it—and many others as well. So that people can become sensitive to the hidden needs of their contemporaries and those numbed in grief can be led back into life, so that current and aspiring pastors are existentially and competently informed for their tasks, and—not least—so that the light of life might shine in the darkness.

—Prof. Dr. Jörg Frey

Bibliography

Aguirre, Regina, and Holli Slater. "Suicide Postvention as Suicide Prevention: Improvement and Expansion in the United States." *Death Studies* 34 (2010) 529–40.

American Psychiatric Association. "Assessing and Treating Suicidal Behaviors: A Quick Reference Guide." https://psychiatryonline.org/pb/assets/raw/sitewide/practice_guidelines/guidelines/suicide-guide.pdf.

———. *Practice Guideline for the Assessment and Treatment of Patients with Suicidal Behaviors.* November 2003. https://psychiatryonline.org/pb/assets/raw/sitewide/practice_guidelines/guidelines/suicide.pdf.

Buber, Martin. *Das dialogische Prinzip: Ich und Du; Zwiesprache; Die Frage an den Einzelnen; Elemente des Zwischenmenschlichen; Zur Geschichte des dialogischen Prinzips.* 17th ed. Gütersloh: Gütersloher, 2017.

Christ-Friedrich, Anna. *Der verzweifelte Versuch zu verändern: Suizidales Handeln als Problem der Seelsorge.* Göttingen: Vandenhoeck & Ruprecht, 1998.

Fechtner, Kristian, et al. *Praktische Theologie: Ein Lehrbuch.* Stuttgart: Kohlhammer, 2017.

Gerlitz, Peter, et al. "Trauer." In *Theologische Realenzyklopädie*, edited by Gerhard Müller, 34:4–27. Berlin: de Gruyter, 2002.

Gill, Peter. *Suizid: Wie weiter? Trauern und Abschiednehmen bei Suizid und plötzlichen Todesfällen.* Basel: Petri, 2014.

Grubitz, Christoph. *Der israelische Aphoristiker Elazar Benyoëtz.* Tübingen: Niemeyer, 1994.

Hausmann, Clemens. *Einführung in die Psychotraumatologie.* Vienna: UTB, 2006.

Herbst, Michael. *Beziehungsweise: Grundlagen und Praxisfelder evangelischer Seelsorge.* 2nd ed. Neukirchen-Vluyn: Neukirchener, 2013.

Hoffmann, John P., ed. *Understanding Religious Ritual: Theoretical Approaches and Innovations.* New York: Routledge, 2014.

Hoheisel, Karl, and Anna Christ-Friedrich. "Suizid." In *Theologische Realenzyklopädie*, edited by Horst Balz et al., 442–53. Berlin: de Gruyter, 2001.

BIBLIOGRAPHY

Horton, Scott. "Hesse's 'In the Fog.'" *Harper's Magazine*, September 22, 2007. https://harpers.org/blog/2007/09/hesses-in-the-fog/.

Kast, Verena. *Trauern: Phasen und Chancen des psychischen Prozesses.* 3rd ed. Freiburg im Breisgau: Kreuz, 2013.

Klessmann, Michael. *Seelsorge: Begleitung, Begegnung, Lebensdeutung im Horizont des christlichen Glaubens; Ein Lehrbuch.* 5th ed. Neukirchen-Vluyn: Neukirchener, 2015.

Koeniger, Georg. *Trauer ist eine lange Reise: Für dich auf den Jakobsweg.* Munich: Piper, 2017.

Kübler-Ross, Elisabeth. *Interviews mit Sterbenden.* Translated by Ulla Leippe. Munich: Knaur, 2001.

Lammer, Kerstin. *Trauer verstehen: Formen, Erklärungen, Hilfen.* 4th ed. Berlin: Springer, 2014.

Lind, Vera. *Selbstmord in der Frühen Neuzeit: Diskurs, Lebenswelt und kultureller Wandel am Beispiel der Herzogtümer Schleswig und Holstein.* Göttingen: Vandenhoeck & Ruprecht, 1999.

Luther, Henning. *Religion und Alltag: Bausteine zu einer Praktischen Theologie des Subjekts.* Stuttgart: Radius, 1992.

Luther, Martin. *Dr. Martin Luthers' sämmtliche Werke: Homiletische und katechetische Schriften.* Edited by Johann Georg Plochmann and Johann Konrad Irmischer. Erlangen: Heyder, 1832.

Meyer-Blanck, Michael, and Birgit Weyel. *Studien- und Arbeitsbuch Praktische Theologie.* Göttingen: Vandenhoeck & Ruprecht, 2008.

Morgenthaler, Christoph. *Seelsorge.* Lehrbuch Praktische Theologie 3. Gütersloh: Gütersloher, 2009.

Nietzsche, Friedrich. *Also sprach Zarathustra.* Hamburg, 2011.

Otzelberger, Manfred. *Suizid: Das Trauma der Hinterbliebenen; Erfahrungen und Auswege.* Munich: Deutscher Taschenbuch, 2002.

"Suicide Act 1961." https://www.legislation.gov.uk/ukpga/Eliz2/9-10/60.

Paul, Chris. *Schuld—Macht—Sinn: Arbeitsbuch für die Begleitung von Schuldfragen im Trauerprozess.* 4th ed. Gütersloh: Gütersloher, 2010.

Plener, Paul L. *Suizidales Verhalten und nichtsuizidale Selbstverletzungen.* Berlin: Springer, 2014.

Rauch, Florian, and Nicole Rinder. *Damit aus Trauma Trauer wird: Weiterleben nach dem Suizid eines nahestehenden Menschen.* Gütersloh: Gütersloher, 2016.

Runeson, Bo, and Marie Åsberg. "Family History of Suicide among Suicide Victims." *American Journal of Psychiatry* 160 (2003) 1525–26.

Schibilsky, Michael. *Trauerwege: Ein Ratgeber für helfende Berufe.* 6th ed. Düsseldorf: Patmos, 2003.

Seidler, Günter H., et al. *Handbuch der Psychotraumatologie.* 2nd ed. Stuttgart: Klett Cotta, 2015.

Spiegel, Yorick. *Der Prozeß des Trauerns: Analyse und Beratung.* Munich: Chr. Kaiser, 1990.

SR 311.0 Schweizerisches Strafgesetzbuch vom 21. December 1937. https://www.admin.ch/opc/de/classified-compilation/19370083/index.html#a111.

Stülpnagel, Freya von. *Warum nur? Trost und Hilfe für Suizid-Hinterbliebene.* Munich: Kösel, 2013.

Wagner, Birgit. *Komplizierte Trauer: Grundlagen, Diagnostik und Therapie.* Berlin: Springer, 2014.

Wittouck, Ciska, et al. "The Prevention and Treatment of Complicated Grief: A Meta-analysis." *Clinical Psychology Review* 31 (2011) 69–78.

Worden, William J. *Grief Counseling and Grief Therapy. A Handbook for the Mental Health Practitioner.* 2nd ed. New York: Springer, 1991.

World Health Organization. *Preventing Suicide: A Global Imperative.* 2014. www.who.int/mental_health/suicide-prevention/world_report_2014/en/.

———. "Suicide." September 2, 2019. www.who.int/mediacentre/factsheets/fs398/en/.

Ziemer, Jürgen. *Seelsorgelehre: Eine Einführung für Studium und Praxis.* 2nd ed. Göttingen: UTB, 2004.